The
INDEPEND...
Coffee Book

— 2012 — EDT^N

LONDON

WORDS BY
Alex Evans

DESIGN BY
Lloyd Price

PHOTOGRAPHY BY
Victor Frankowski

café

moulu

ORSICA

CAFÉ CÔTE S

100%

CAFÉ C
GRA

POIDS N

First published in the UK by Vespertine Press 2011

Copyright © Vespertine Press 2011
Text © A.J. Evans
except page 96 © Derek Lamberton
Photography © Victor Frankowski

A catalogue record of this book is available from
the British Library

ISBN 978-0-9566582-2-7

Cover & layout design by L.V. Price

Printed & bound in the UK by Four Corners Print

Printed on paper produced by sustainably managed forests.

Set in **TR Avalon**, **U.S. 101** &
Wisdom Script – courtesy of James T Edmondson.

Also available from Vespertine Press -
The Brighton & Hove Independent Café Guide

www.independentcafes.co.uk

CONTENTS

East

North

South

CONTENTS CONTINUED OVERLEAF

USING THIS GUIDE

The first part of this book serves as a guide to the best cafés and coffee houses in London. They are divided into five key areas comprising *The City, The West End, East, North* and *South,* allowing you to easily find places depending on your location.

There are three page styles distinguishing cafés, coffee carts and roasters, each containing key information including opening hours and nearest train and bus stops, as well as listing what's on offer at each location such as coffee options, facilities and outdoor seating. (Please note, bus information only denotes services to the nearest stop. Some cafés may be served by alternative routes.)

The second part of this book is a coffee compendium comprising information about coffee, its history and its place in the world today. Finally, at the back of the book you will find maps for all of the cafés and carts featured in the guide.

The following logos appear throughout the guide. They represent:

 Coffee Roaster    Coffee Cart    KeepCup Stockist

KEEPCUP. THE WORLD'S FIRST BARISTA STANDARD REUSABLE CUP

Since product launch in June 2009, KeepCup has become Australia's leading reusable cup, sold by many of the most respected names in coffee. KeepCups have kick started positive behaviour change from discard to reuse that is gaining momentum around the world.

While operating in the café industry, sister and brother, Abigail and Jamie Forsyth observed the lack of choice for consumers wanting to use a well designed commuter cup for espresso coffee.

"We took a big gamble that usability and aesthetics were key reasons for poor take up of reusables as alternatives to disposable cups. People purchase the KeepCup because they want to be sustainable, but they keep using them because they love the way they look and feel."

KeepCup aims to support and encourage a change in the way people on the move enjoy their takeaway coffee. Many small acts can make a phenomenal difference.

WHEN THE KEEPCUP LOGO APPEARS IN THIS BOOK IT MEANS KEEPCUPS ARE USED AND SOLD AT THE CAFE. MANY CAFES GIVE A DISCOUNT FOR USING A REUSABLE CUP.

PRODUCT FEATURES:

— Lightweight, portable, unbreakable.
— Dishwasher safe (top drawer).
— Fits under the group heads of most espresso machines.
— Replicates disposable cup sizes.
— Lift and twist plug to open breather hole and drinking hole.
— BPA free. Non toxic.
— Polypropylene #5. Food safe.
— Award winning sustainable product design.
— Warranted for one year, we estimate it will last four.

BETTER & BETTER
KEEPCUP.COM

FOREWORD

By
Nick & Andrew Jolley

TAYLOR ST. BARISTAS

London's coffee has come a long way. As little as five years ago, you could count on one hand the number of cafés that sold a quality coffee. Today, we are spoilt for choice. In fact, we are so spoilt for choice that, these days, London's coffee scene is increasingly counted amongst the most vibrant in the world.

London's emergence as a standard bearer in the world of quality coffee owes much to the passion and skills of those involved at each of the steps in the chain, from the producer to the cup. So often as coffee consumers, we're infatuated with the skills and expertise of the higher profile parts of this chain: the boutique roasters and the rockstar baristas. Yet all their work would count for nothing if it weren't for the dedication of the growers, processing mills and importers that fuel their craft. Critically, London is blessed with access to some of the world's best 'specialty grade' coffee, and it is this that lays the foundation for our quality coffee scene.

The specialty grade coffee that lands in England is grown throughout the equatorial belt. It ripens in origin countries at different times in the year, meaning there are windows in time when coffees from different producing countries are seen to shine. As a result, we have access to seasonal coffees at their prime nearly all year round. The coffee is then roasted in small batches by hand to discover and unlock the flavours hidden within the beans. More than eight hundred discernible flavours have been identified in coffees from around the globe, representing a treasure trove of opportunity for the skilled artisanal roaster. The roasted coffee is then carefully packaged to delay degradation as a myriad of factors - including light, moisture, high temperatures and oxygen - conspire to ruin the roaster's handiwork.

It's only after all this toil that London's baristas are presented with the opportunity to display their craft. Keeping in mind that a single coffee tree produces as little as 500g of roasted coffee each season, this is a precious privilege indeed. A slight lapse in concentration, worn grinder burrs or a less than ideal water supply can ruin the coffee that has travelled so far. Luckily, London is blessed with a growing cadre of skilled baristas who are knowledgeable enough - and passionate enough - to present the coffees as they should be.

One of the reasons London's cafés are up there with the best in the world is their commitment to the flavours of the coffee and finding the best way to get them into the cup. The cafés presented in this guide will let you taste, savour and salivate over the richness of the world's best.

The City

The City, also known as the Square Mile, is home to London's major financial institutions and is the nation's hub for big business. It has also been coffee's spiritual London home since 1652, when the city's very first coffee house began trading in Cornhill. Some of the original coffee house sites still remain over three hundred years later, standing testaments to Old London's oft overlooked coffee heritage. Bounded by Islington in the north, Commercial Street in the East, the river to the South and Holborn to the West, the area today has continued its pioneering coffee theme and is home to some of the capital's most high-profile coffee shops.

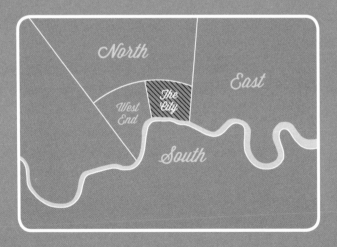

PRUFROCK COFFEE

23-25 Leather Lane EC1N 7TE
www.prufrockcoffee.com

Hours - Mon-Fri: 7 - 6
             Sat: 10 - 4

Trains - Chancery Lane /
             Farringdon Tube

Buses - Routes 17, 341, 45, 46
            Holborn Circus

Loyalty Card - No

Wi-Fi - Yes

Alcohol - No

W.C. - Yes

Outdoor Seating - No

Machine - Nuova Simonelli *Aurelia*   **Beans** - Square Mile

Grinders - Mazzer *Robur E*, Mahlkönig *Tanzania*

Alternative Brewing Methods - Syphon, Pour Over, AeroPress

Prufrock Leather Lane is founder Gwilym Davies's grandest and most benevolent project to date and has rapidly become both a stronghold for the company and yet another achievement to add to his already impressive list of coffee acumen.

Gwilym's triumph in the 2009 World Barista Championships was not only the catalyst for his or Prufrock's fortunes, but also for many of the positive changes in the coffee industry in the last half-decade. Since then he has been a vocal advocate of better practice within the industry and a tireless ambassador for London's coffee movement. With Prurock Leather Lane, both he and co-director Jeremy Challender have created a café in which to bring together their ample experience, not only to maintain the exceptional standard of coffee Prufrock has always offered, but also to provide a venue in which to help educate London's new breed of professional baristas.

Worlds apart from Gwilym's Columbia Road coffee cart or the Prufrock concession within Shoreditch menswear store Present, the space itself is huge, punctuated by minimalist designer chairs offset by worn floorboards and reclaimed wooden benches. The centrepiece is the ample brew bar which played host to the U.K. Brewers Cup in 2011 and is home to all manner of coffee gadgetry and brewing equipment, like the *Über* boiler and the glowing halogen beam heaters that make the visual performance of the syphon filter all the more enjoyable. Indeed, it seems that Prufrock's premise is to make your stay simultaneously fun and educational, feeling like a contemporary homage to brewing and invention, where coffee is made by a team of young, highly skilled baristas who look set to follow in the footsteps of their pre-eminent employers.

The 10,000 Hours sign that hangs on the wall beside the stairwell, points below ground to the affectionately named London *BRAT*, Prufrock's very own Barista Resource and Training area. Running interactive, hands-on classes on espresso, latte art, brew methods and coffee tasting, overseen by some of London's finest baristas, not to mention Gwilym and Jeremy themselves, this is an ideal place for the budding coffee geek or brewer to learn from some bona fide coffee royalty. It is also evidence of Prufrock's stoical commitment to both raising awareness and understanding of coffee and to sharing what they have in an open, accessible forum. Built on past successes and years of knowledge, Prufrock's sights seem firmly set on ensuring a healthy future for specialty coffee in the capital.

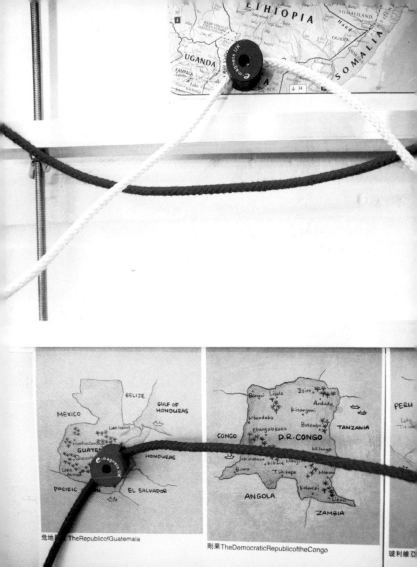

危地 TheRepublicofGuatemala

剛果TheDemocraticRepublicoftheCongo

CARAVAN

11-13 Exmouth Market EC1R 4QD
www.caravanonexmouth.co.uk
T. 0207 833 8115

The City

Hours - Mon-Fri: 8 - 10.30
        Sat: 10 - 10.30
        Sun: 10 - 4

Trains - Farringdon Tube

Buses - Routes 341, 19, 38
        Mount Pleasant

Loyalty Card - Yes

Wi-Fi - Yes

Alcohol - Yes

W.C. - Yes

Outdoor Seating - No

Machine - La Marzocco *Linea*   Beans - Caravan

Grinders - Mazzer *Robur E*, Anfim *Super Caimano*

Alternative Brewing Methods - Pour Over, AeroPress

With its name and essence derived from the personal and professional journeys that its owners have embarked upon, Caravan carries all the hallmarks of the experience and expertise garnered upon their individual travels, culminating in the creation of their very own New Zealand-style café.

Though unconventional in café terms - incorporating both a well stocked bar and a gourmet restaurant - Caravan's strong food focus and wine list does nothing to detract from their aptitude for coffee. From their adapted basement, small batches of ethically sourced green coffees are roasted daily to create a unique Caravan espresso blend that is served both in the café upstairs and to wholesale customers across London. Situated on the south-west corner of Exmouth Market, Caravan really springs to life in the warmer months when its sliding doors are opened wide and the sights, smells and sounds of the café blend harmoniously with the bustle of the street market outside.

ST. ALI

27 Clerkenwell Road EC1M 5RN
T. 0207 253 5754
www.stali.co.uk

The City

Hours - Mon-Sun: 7 - 6

Trains - Farringdon Tube

Buses - Routes 153, 243, 55
Clerkenwell Road

Loyalty Card - No

Wi-Fi - No

Alcohol - Yes

W.C. - Yes

Outdoor Seating - Yes

Machines - Slayer, Synesso *Cyncra*   Beans - St. Ali, Square Mile,
                                                Has Bean
Grinders - Mazzer *Robur E* & *Super Jolly*

Alternative Brewing Methods - Pour Over, AeroPress

Even before St. Ali arrived in Clerkenwell in Spring 2011, talk of their imminent launch was rife in the capital. The reason for such mass conjecture was based upon St. Ali's reputation as one of Melbourne's foremost coffee companies, having been established in 2005 amidst fierce competition for supremacy in arguably the toughest coffee market in the world. The company's first foray overseas speaks as much about their desire to participate in exciting new territories as it does London's reputation as one of the world's up and coming coffee cities.

The two and a half thousand square feet café/roastery is a masterpiece of modern, industrial styling with an expansive counter and brew bar laden with coffee technology. Furthermore, the living wall of plants and flowers that scales the brickwork adjacent to the fully integrated, on site roasting facility both spell out St. Ali's grandiose intentions.

However, despite the initial enchantment created by such big budget aesthetics, the longer lasting impression that St. Ali creates is retained in the finer details. The warm greeting and attentive service, the milk bottles that serve as water decanters and their delicately prepared filter coffees are all clearly considered, lending a quality and comfort to your stays not often found outside of high-end hospitality. The upstairs restaurant area is a draw in its own right, boasting an extensive menu steeped in Australian café goodness such as banana bread, corn fritters and poached eggs on sourdough toast, alongside a list of fine wines and ales from London's renowned Kernel Brewery, just in case the pick-me-up you require extends further than the coffee.

With its name inspired by one of coffee history's semi-mythical patron saints, the expert attention applied to all things coffee will ultimately set St. Ali apart in a city already teeming with fine food options. St. Ali's 'Director of Coffee' Tim Styles has a list of credentials to match anyone in the business, having worked for the company in Melbourne before stints at Intelligentsia in the US and London heavyweights Square Mile and Flat White. The glowing reviews of sister project Sensory Lab in Marylebone are testament to the company's dedication to coffee exploration and expect to see blends like their *Cult of Done* espresso gracing coffee menus across the city as their U.K. roasting division hits its stride. For once, the hype certainly seems justified.

DOSE ESPRESSO

70 Long Lane EC1A 9EJ
www.dose-espresso.com
T. 0207 600 0382

The City

Hours - Mon-Fri: 7 - 4 Sat: 9 - 1	**Loyalty Card** - Yes
	Wi-Fi - No
Trains - Barbican / Farringdon Tube	**Alcohol** - No
	W.C. - No
Buses - Routes 56 , 153, 4 Barbican Station	**Outdoor Seating** - Yes

Machine - La Marzocco *FB-80*   **Beans** - Square Mile

Grinders - Anfim *Super Caimano & Best*, Mahlkönig *Vario*

Alternative Brewing Methods - AeroPress, Clever Dripper

When it opened in early 2009, Dose was one of the first Antipodean inspired, coffee-focused cafés in London and, despite its diminutive dimensions and the ensuing flood of high-grade coffee shops that have followed, Dose has held its own, and with good reason. Kiwi proprietor James Phillips had worked in the Sydney coffee business for seven years before moving to London and ran the Climpson & Sons stall on Broadway Market for two years before using his ample experience to focus on Dose. Square Mile's seasonal espresso blends are served alongside guest coffees from a rotating order of the U.K.'s finest roasters and there is also a coffee selected weekly to showcase as either espresso or Aeropress. As an independent, Dose also sees ethical practices as essential and relies on quality local suppliers, such as the highly acclaimed Bittersweet Bakes, for all their delicious cakes. In brief, Dose is a small piece of London real estate with an excellent and hugely deserved reputation.

LOOK MUM NO HANDS!

49 Old Street EC1V 9HX
T. 0207 253 1025
www.lookmumnohands.com

Hours - Mon-Fri: 7.30 - 10
Sat: 9 - 10
Sun: 10 - 10

Trains - Barbican / Old St. Tube

Buses - Routes 55, 243
Aldersgate Street

Loyalty Card - Yes

Wi-Fi - Yes

Alcohol - Yes

W.C. - Yes

Outdoor Seating - Yes

Machine - La Marzocco *Linea*

Grinder - Anfim *Super Caimano*

Beans - Square Mile

A haven for both bike and coffee enthusiasts alike, Look Mum No Hands! rode up in 2010 and has already become a focal point for the Old Street community. Their bike repair workshop, open daily from 7.30am to 8pm, can provide running repairs whilst you wait and organizes a monthly bike jumble attended by velophiles from all over the city. Indeed, the café is at its most vibrant during the summer months when the Tour De France is shown on their projector screen, the walls are draped with Tricolour bunting and bikes of all descriptions hang and rest at every available space and line the streets nearby.

Thankfully the good people here have as much of a passion for coffee and food as they do for two wheeled transport. Using Square Mile's espresso blends, coffees are pulled to order by accomplished baristas whilst the menu consists of pies, salads and a wholesome specials board. The fridges are also well stocked with Suffolk Cider, Bath Ales and Belgian beers, perfect after a long day pedaling.

GIDDY UP

Fortune Street Park EC1Y
twitter.com/GiddyUpCoffee

Hours - Mon-Fri: 8 - 4.30
Sat & Sun: 10 - 4

Trains - Barbican / Old St. Tube

Buses - Routes 153, 4, 56
Barbican Station

Machine - La Marzocco *GB/5*

Grinder - Anfim *Super Caimano*

Beans - Square Mile, Has Bean

Alongside having one of the all-time best names for a coffee cart, Giddy Up also has one of the nicest locations, set-up amidst the pleasant environs of the Fortune Street Park, which is closer to the City's major thoroughfares than the relative quietude suggests. Giddy Up also has the good fortune of being owned and run by two extremely talented and affable individuals. Lee Harte is a relative London old timer, having previously worked at Flat Cap, Tina, We Salute You and Whitecross Street coffee cart just around the corner, whilst Alice Cooke is herself no coffee novice, having finished sixth in the 2011 U.K. Barista Championships. With such experienced professionals at the helm, expect not only excellent coffee but also the hardy, all-weathers sense of humour only found in those accustomed to 8am starts and the demands of pouring latte art with frostbitten fingers. Thankfully for Lee and Alice, Giddy Up will soon be operating from within the warmth and shelter of the hut next door which should only make the duo more genial, if indeed that's possible.

TAYLOR ST. BARISTAS

Unit 3, 125 Old Broad St. EC2N 1AR
www.taylor-st.com

Hours - Mon-Fri: 7 - 5

Trains - Bank Tube & DLR /
Liverpool St. Tube & Rail

Buses - Routes 8,26,242,388,11,23,133
Old Broad Street

Loyalty Card - Yes

Wi-Fi - Yes

Alcohol - No

W.C. - No

Outdoor Seating - No

Machines - Nuova Simonelli *Aurelia*
Synesso *Hydra*
Grinders - 3x Anfim *Super Caimano*
2x Mazzer *Robur E*
Alternative Brewing Methods - AeroPress, Cloth Filter

Beans - Union
Square Mile
James Gourmet
Has Bean

Having grown weary of the bleak English weather and the meagreness of coffee options available in the U.K., the Aussie sibling trio of Nick, Andrew and Laura Tolley could have given up and returned to the fairer climate and evolved café culture of their homeland. But instead they made it their mission to help raise the standard of coffee in London and from opening their first café back in 2006, Taylor St. venues and their stellar reputation have since multiplied.

In the heart of London's financial district and just a few streets away from the site of the city's oldest coffee house on Saint Michael's Alley, Taylor St. Barista's flagship Bank café has been serving up expertly crafted coffee since 2010. Packed with cutting edge equipment, Taylor St. Bank peaks at lunchtime when scores of besuited regulars take their much needed out-of-office coffee breaks and the ample café becomes akin to a coffee factory, with baristas and espresso machines working in near seamless conjunction.

Although Taylor St. carry a regularly updated list of guest espresso and single origin coffees, their house *Rogue* espresso blend is the mainstay of the coffee menu and was developed in collaboration between Union Hand-Roasted and Taylor St.'s very own Andrew Tolley. Designed to be an unconventional and ever changing blend, *Rogue*'s components are adjusted to incorporate some of the best seasonal lots, but is kept sweet and balanced in the roast and then consistently extracted by baristas throughout their cafés. It means that whether joining the coffee queue that trails from the doorway of the New Street café, lunching in their swish Mayfair outlet or enjoying the unusual surrounds of what can only be described as their Shoreditch coffee 'shed', you can be sure that whenever you see Taylor St.'s name, the coffee you receive will be consistently high-grade.

The gradual upscale of their business, which now features seven individual cafés across London, has allowed the formation of Taylor St.'s very own state-of-the-art barista training school in Monument, where new coffee recruits hone their skills and their already battle-hardened baristas can perfect their art. Despite such steady growth and popularity, Taylor St. is still owned and run by the brother and sister team who established it and still maintains its ethos of striving for better. In the ever changing London coffee industry, where independent cafes can run the risk of getting left behind or expanding at such a rate that their product suffers, Taylor St.'s steady upward trajectory is testament to hard work, talent and a passion for coffee that, when combined, is both a formidable partnership and a benchmark for others.

FLAT CAP COFFEE CO. (FLEET STREET)

186 Fleet Street EC4A 2HR
www.notesmusiccoffee.com
Opening Hours: Mon-Fri: 8 - 4.30
Trains: Chancery Lane / Temple Tube
Buses: 11, 15, 172, 23, 26, 341 - Chancery Lane

DEPARTMENT OF COFFEE & SOCIAL AFFAIRS

14 - 16 Leather Lane EC1N 7SU
www.departmentofcoffee.co.uk
Opening Hours: Mon-Fri: 7.30 - 5 Sat & Sun: 10 - 4
Trains: Chancery Lane / Farringdon Tube
Buses: 17, 341, 45, 46 - Holborn Circus / Fetter Lane

FARM COLLECTIVE

91 Cowcross Street, Farringdon EC1M 6BH
www.farmcollective.com
Opening Hours: Mon-Fri: 7 - 3.30
Trains: Farringdon Tube
Buses: 17, 45, 46, 63 - Snow Hill

BEA'S OF BLOOMSBURY (ST. PAULS)

One New Change, 83 Watling Street EC4M 9BX
www.beasofbloomsbury.com
Opening Hours: Mon-Fri: 7 - 7 Sat & Sun: 12 - 7
Trains: St. Paul's Tube
Buses: 100, 172, 4, 521 - New Change / Cannon Street

FIX COFFEE

161 Whitecross Street EC1Y 8JL
www.fix-coffee.co.uk
Opening Hours: Mon-Fri: 7 - 7 Sat & Sun: 8 - 7
Trains: Old Street Rail & Tube
Buses: 55, 243 - St. Luke's

THE SHOREDITCH GRIND

213 Old Street EC1V 9NR
www.shoreditchgrind.com
Opening Hours: Mon-Fri: 7 - 8 Sat: 9 - 7 Sun: 10 - 6
Trains: Old Street Rail & Tube
Buses: 135, 205, 214, 43 - Old Street Roundabout

TAYLOR ST. BARISTAS (SHOREDITCH)

110 Clifton Street, Shoreditch EC2A 4HT
www.taylor-st.com
Opening Hours: Mon-Fri: 8 - 5
Trains: Shoreditch High Street Rail & Tube
Buses: 35, 47, 78 - Curtain Road

TAYLOR ST. BARISTAS (NEW STREET)

1A New Street EC2M 4TP
www.taylor-st.com
Opening Hours: Mon-Fri: 7 - 5 Sun: 10 - 4
Trains: Liverpool Street Rail & Tube
Buses: 149, 344, 35, 47, 48 - Liverpool St. Station

West End

During the 17th Century, the West End's most famous historical coffee house was *Will's*, situated on Russell Street in Covent Garden. Since then, London's West End has always been synonymous with the glamorous upper classes, who have consistently flocked to its famous theatres, restaurants and high-end bars. Today, the West End comprises some of the city's foremost tourist attractions such as Trafalgar Square, Piccadilly Circus and Covent Garden, and is home to London's most famous art galleries. The area also incorporates neighbourhoods as far West as Hyde Park, including Soho, Fitzrovia and the premier shopping destination of Oxford Street.

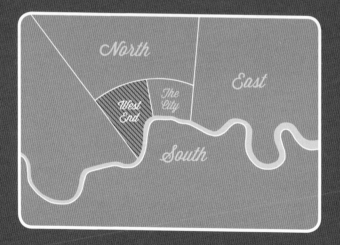

TAPPED & PACKED

26 Rathbone Place, Fitzrovia W1T 1JD
T. 0207 580 2163
www.tappedandpacked.co.uk

West End

Hours - Mon-Fri: 8 - 7
Sat: 10 - 6

Trains - Goodge St. / Tottenham
Court Rd Tube

Buses - Routes 10,134,14,24,29,390,73
Percy Street

Loyalty Card - No

Wi-Fi - Yes

Alcohol - No

W.C. - No

Outdoor Seating - Yes

Machine - La Marzocco *GB/5*

Grinders - Anfim *Super Caimano*,
Mazzer *Robur E & Super Jolly*

Alternative Brewing Methods - AeroPress, V60

Beans - Square Mile
Climpson's
Has Bean
Union
Origin Coffee

keep cup

Marked only by the number 26 on the shop front and the vintage delivery bicycle stationed outside, Tapped & Packed's first coffee shop has arisen as a West End trailblazer which stands out from even the area's most prestigious specialty coffee shops. Its interior is a contemporary, rustic amalgam of timber boards, a zinc fronted counter, suede benches and chunky wooden tables, topped off with sugar served from Tate and Lyle syrup cans and an array of antique demitasse spoons. The Belfast sink by the front window is piled with crushed ice to cool drinks bottles, fruits and bowls of Bircher muesli, whilst the counter displays an array of freshly made sandwiches and choice confection.

Tapped & Packed has been one of the few London cafés to promote the diversity of coffee via a list of single origin beans from the U.K.'s finest artisanal roasters, including the likes of Union Hand-Roasted, Has Bean, Square Mile and East London's Climpson & Sons. Their ever-changing menu of filter options from around the world are brewed in drip filters or AeroPress by baristas who are themselves immersed in the delicate art of coffee. If coffee isn't your cup of tea, Tapped & Packed offers a fourteen-strong list of teas and infusions from the renowned Postcard Teas, which, like their coffees, are all chosen with the highest standards in mind.

The newest addition to Tapped & Packed's armoury is a second café at number 114 Tottenham Court Road which may be more diminutive but nonetheless carries all the hallmarks of its older sibling. The bicycle suspended above the doorway, the attractive scattering of drop lights and the quality of coffee it achieves have all become hallmarks of the company and motifs that are flatteringly replicated in other aspiring cafés. In their design and the underlying attitude of quality without compromise, Tapped & Packed's coffee shops encapsulate the cutting edge cool of London's newest generation of coffee lovers, baristas and the city's exuberant café culture.

THE ESPRESSO ROOM

31-35 Great Ormond Street WC1N 3HZ
www.theespressoroom.com

Hours - Mon-Fri: 7.30 - 5
Sat: 9.30 - 2.30

Trains - Russell Square Tube

Buses - Routes 19, 243, 38, 55
Red Lion Square

Loyalty Card - Yes

Wi-Fi - No

Alcohol - No

W.C. - No

Outdoor Seating - Yes

Machine - La Marzocco *Linea*

Grinders - Mazzer *Robur E*, Mahlkönig *Tanzania*
Baratza *Vario* x 2

Alternative Brewing Methods - French Press, Pour Over

Beans - Square Mile
Has Bean

Situated opposite the site of Great Ormond Street Hospital, the queue and sweet coffee aroma that often extend from Espresso Room's doorway have been commonplace now since 2009. Its name is about as literal as they come – a single room café whose coffee focus is second to none - but the Espresso Room has transcended the narrow confines of its site to become something of a landmark in London.

The espresso blend that provides the foundation for their award winning beverages comes from Square Mile, whilst they also offer guest coffees from Has Bean, prepared as a French press or filter. Owner Ben Townsend is a hugely knowledgeable member of the capital's coffee fraternity and one of only a select few who runs workshops and training courses at the London School of Coffee, giving others the chance to learn the secrets of his success.

STORE ST. ESPRESSO

40 Store Street WC1E 7DB
www.twitter.com/storestespresso

Hours - Mon-Fri: 8 - 7
        Sat: 9 - 7

Trains - Goodge St. Tube

Buses - Routes 10, 134, 14, 24, 29
        Chenies Street

Loyalty Card - Yes

Wi-Fi - Yes

Alcohol - No

W.C. - Yes

Outdoor Seating - Yes

Machine - La Marzocco *Linea*

Grinder - Anfim *Super Caimano*

Beans - Square Mile

Some cafés have a spec that reads like a checklist of 'must haves' – top of the range espresso machine, expertly roasted coffee, sleek industrial styling and reclaimed furniture... but far from guaranteeing a café's success, such components can merely provide the platform upon which to apply expertise, warmth of service and technical skills.

However, on the leafy Bloomsbury street from which it garners its name, Store St. Espresso is one of the few that has it all. The deceptively spacious interior is an archetypal modern and minimalist space, with concrete floors and wooden tables that are bathed in light from an impressive central skylight. Neat, simple and quiet, which is something that cannot be said for many central London cafés, Store St. is an much-utilised reading corner for students. The café's popularity is made all the more impressive given that it shares a locality with several of London's big hitters, which proves that the coffee they serve is up there with the best of their illustrious neighbours.

LANTANA

13-14 Charlotte Place, Fitzrovia W1T 1SN
T. 0207 637 3347
www.lantanacafe.co.uk

Hours - Mon-Fri: 8 - 6
         Sat & Sun: 9 - 5

Trains - Goodge Street Tube

Buses - Routes 10,134,14,24,29,390,73
        Goodge Street Station

Loyalty Card - Yes

Wi-Fi - Yes

Alcohol - Yes

W.C. - Yes

Outdoor Seating - Yes

Machine - La Marzocco *Linea*

Grinders - Anfim *Milano*, Mazzer *Super Jolly*

Beans - Square Mile

Brisbanite Shelagh Ryan opened Lantana with the express intention of bringing a piece of Australia to a pretty side street of Fitzrovia, a seemingly modest mission statement but not when you consider the incredible standard of coffee and café cuisine to be found in parts of the Southern Hemisphere. In order to maintain Lantana's brief, Shelagh and her team provide a menu dripping with sumptuous, Aussie-style brunch and lunch options, such as Lantana toasted banana bread, baked eggs and chorizo sausage and warm poached fruit served with vanilla crème fraiche and crushed pistachios. Alike the menu, in order to keep up with Southern Hemisphere standards, coffee is roasted by the experts at Square Mile and prepared by a talented crew of baristas.

      The name Lantana refers to a hardy plant that flourishes in unlikely environments and since opening in 2008, the café has certainly blossomed, much like the beautiful mural of flowers that graces the back wall of the café, becoming a home-from-home for legions of London's Aussie ex-pats.

KAFFEINE

66 Great Titchfield Street, Fitzrovia W1W 7QJ
T. 0207 580 6755
www.kaffeine.co.uk

Hours - Mon-Fri: 7.30 - 6
        Sat: 9 - 6
        Sun: 9.30 - 5

Trains - Oxford Circus /
         Tottenham Ct. Rd Tube

Buses - Routes 12, 3, 453, 88, C2
        Margaret Street

Loyalty Card - No

Wi-Fi - No

Alcohol - No

W.C. - Yes

Outdoor Seating - Yes

Machine - Synesso *Cyncra*

Grinder - Mazzer *Robur E*

Beans - Square Mile

Another of Fitzrovia's favourite Aussie-style cafés is the illustrious Kaffeine, whose owner Peter Dore-Smith has drawn on all his twenty years of industry experience in Australia and the U.K. to create this perfectly formed homage to coffee. The William Tozer designed interior of minimalist pine, slatted boxes, a bluestone bar and exposed brickwork provides a tranquil environment that contrasts the bustle of nearby Oxford Street. Kaffeine's baristas all have a wealth of experience of their own and their expertise behind the awesome Synesso that takes pride of place upon the counter has drawn mighty accolades and awards in recent years. All of their foodstuffs are produced on site with ingredients sourced from local vendors, specialist suppliers and independent market traders and there is the added bonus of an office catering menu that is updated weekly via their blog in line with market produce and seasonality. Now an established name on the radar of London's most discerning coffee junkies, Kaffeine is a must visit for anyone who has yet to sample its ample Australasian charms.

NUDE ESPRESSO

19 Soho Square W1D 3QN
T. 07804 223590
www.nudeespresso.com

Hours - Mon-Fri: 8 - 5
        Sat & Sun: 11 - 6

Trains - Tottenham Ct. Rd Tube

Buses - Routes 10,25,390,55,7,73,8,98
        Oxford Street / Soho Street

Loyalty Card - No

Wi-Fi - No

Alcohol - No

W.C. - No

Outdoor Seating - Yes

Machine - Nude modified Wega *Nova*   Beans - Nude

Grinder - Wega *68mm Konic*

Alternative Brewing Methods - Aeropress, Pour Over

Having virtually cornered the coffee market around Brick Lane with their café and roasting division, Nude makes its first foray into the West side of the city with their vision of a 21st century espresso bar. Their third outlet marks a step up into the big league of London's coffee elite, and the sleek finish of its interior design is cutting edge, in keeping with the glamour of its Soho Square address. The gleaming roaster, that serves as a novel window dressing, also alludes to their Truman Brewery roastery, which now not only services their Hanbury Street café but provides their ever present *East* espresso blend and a selection of single origin and micro-lot coffees for their latest Soho hangout. Food options are small but delicious, consisting of sandwiches, pastries and Antipodean treats, like their much coveted chocolate lamingtons. However, this Kiwi success story is all down to a love of coffee, exemplified by the awning out front which is emblazoned with Nude's motto - 'Respect the Bean'.

MILKBAR

3 Bateman Street, Soho W1D 4AG
T. 0207 287 4796
www.flatwhitecafe.com

Hours - Mon-Fri: 8 - 7
Sat & Sun: 9 - 6

Trains - Tottenham Court Rd. /
Leicester Sq. Tube

Buses - Routes 14, 19, 38
Gerrard Pl. / Chinatown

Loyalty Card - Yes

Wi-Fi - No

Alcohol - No

W.C. - No

Outdoor Seating - Yes

Machine - La Marzocco *FB/80*

Grinders - Mazzer *Robur E* & *Super Jolly*

Beans - Square Mile

A milk bar is a term used in Australia to describe a local convenience store, and the loyal custom shown this prime West End coffee spot is comparable to that afforded the humble neighbourhood shop, even if their main draw is caffeine as opposed a loaf of bread or the daily paper. Tucked away from the main Soho thoroughfares, Milkbar is brighter and more spacious than its older sibling Flat White, making it a popular alternative for those who prefer to take a little time over their coffee break. However, with its beaten floorboards, black walls and leather benches, the interior is as similarly understated as its predecessor.

During London's coffee uprising over the past few years, where cafés have been hasty in scaling up their operations, the Flat White/Milkbar model has kept its feet reassuringly on the ground. Having held on to a hardcore of talented baristas and staff since opening its doors back in 2008, the team consistently pull some of the best espresso in London whilst all the while maintaining their regular, effortless cool.

FLAT WHITE

17 Berwick Street, Soho W1F 0PT
T. 0207 734 0370
www.flatwhitecafe.com

Hours - Mon-Fri: 8.30 - 7
        Sat & Sun: 9 - 6

Trains - Tottenham Court Rd. /
         Picadilly Circus Tube

Buses - Routes 25, 55, 7, 98
        Wardour Street

Loyalty Card - Yes

Wi-Fi - No

Alcohol - No

W.C. - No

Outdoor Seating - Yes

Machine - Synesso *Hydra*

Grinders - Mazzer *Robur E* & *Super Jolly*

Beans - Square Mile

No guide to London cafés would be complete without the inclusion of Berwick Street's very own coffee institution. With a reputation for being one of the capital's primary purveyors of speciality coffee culture, Flat White rocked up in 2005 and has become somewhat of a mecca for coffee lovers the world over. In the years since Flat White opened, the drink from which its name is derived has become commonplace nomenclature, though very few coffee shops in London still make them quite as expertly. If you're in any doubt as to how the perfect 'flattie' should taste, never fear - Flat White boasts some of the city's finest barista talent behind the huge custom Synesso that resides on the counter and their coffee never fails to disappoint. With such success comes the obvious clamour for seats but if there happens to be a premium on space inside, there is never any shortage of entertainment outside on Berwick Street Market, which has been another of Soho's attractions since the eighteenth century.

FERNANDEZ & WELLS

73 Beak Street, Soho W1F 9SR
T. 0207 287 8124
www.fernandezandwells.com

Hours - Mon-Fri: 7.30 - 6
       Sat: 9 - 6
       Sun: 9 - 5

Trains - Picadilly Circus /
       Oxford Circus Tube

Buses - Routes 13, 139, 15, 23, 6
       Conduit St. / Hamley's

Loyalty Card - No

Wi-Fi - Yes

Alcohol - No

W.C. - Yes

Outdoor Seating - No

Machine - Synesso *Hydra*

Grinders - Mazzer *Robur E & Super Jolly*

Beans - F&W blend by
       Has Bean

The trademark design features that greet you on entering any of Jorge Fernandez and Rick Wells' three Soho venues have set a visual benchmark that many other London cafés have attempted to imitate, though recreating the finer trappings of Fernandez & Well's success is not quite as straightforward. Inspired by the Slow Food Movement and a wealth of experience gathered whilst working for big names such as Monmouth Coffee, F & W have set about providing produce and drinks sourced from a carefully selected assortment of specialist companies, such as Has Bean who roast their custom espresso blend and the Flour Station for their artisanal breads. Their Beak Street café has become a firm favourite of the Soho lunch crowd, who form orderly queues for the mouth-watering focaccia sandwiches and baguettes. The food and wine bar round the corner on Lexington Street caters for slightly more refined food palates, whilst their little espresso bar on St. Anne's Court is perfect for a quick caffeine stop. All come highly recommended.

NOTES MUSIC & COFFEE

31 St. Martin's Lane, Covent Garden WC2N 4ER
T. 0207 240 0424
www.notesmusiccoffee.com

West End

Hours - Mon&Tue: 7.30 - 9
Wed-Fri: 7.30 - 10
Sat: 9 - 10   Sun: 10 - 7

Trains - Charing Cross /
Leicester Square Tube

Buses - Routes 176, 24, 29
St. Martin's Place

Loyalty Card - No

Wi-Fi - No

Alcohol - Yes

W.C. - Yes

Outdoor Seating - Yes

Machine - La Marzocco *Strada*

Grinders - Mahlkönig *Vario*, Mazzer *Robur E* &
Super Jolly

Beans - Square Mile, Has Bean

Alternative Brewing Methods - Aeropress, V60, Syphon,
Woodneck, Eva Solo

Fabio Ferreira's father and grandfather worked as coffee farmers in his native Brazil, but Note's co-owner and head barista was only compelled to enter the coffee industry himself after visiting London eight years ago. He then trained as a barista and established the Flat Cap Coffee cart with Robert Robinson before they opened Notes in late 2010. Inside, this looks and feels like a no-expense-spared project; the perfect stage for Fabio to practice the art of coffee making and exercise his abundant charm. A stool at the brew bar is the best position to sample one of the various single origin coffees they serve on rotation. Underneath a vaulted skylight at the back of the café there is ample seating and downstairs there are racks of classical, jazz and blues CDs providing the laid back music the drifts melodiously around the room. Notes is also open later than most, making it an ideal venue for some pre-theatre downtime.

FLAT CAP COFFEE CO.

**4 Strutton Ground, Victoria Street
Westminster SW1P 2HR**

Hours - Mon-Fri: 8 - 4.30
        Sat & Sun: 10 - 4

Trains - St James's Park /
         Victoria Tube

Buses - Routes 11, 148, 211, 24
        New Scotand Yard

Machine - La Marzocco *GB/5*

Grinders - Anfim *Super Caimano*
           Gaggia *MD-58*

Beans - Square Mile

F lat Cap's most famous outpost on Strutton ground is the flagship of an ever growing fleet of specialty coffee carts. Owned and operated by the team behind Covent Garden's ever popular Notes Music and Coffee, the cart was established as a first coffee venture by Fabio Ferreira and never fails to produce coffees of the highest order. Akin to its sister cart stationed on Fleet Street, the stand is tastefully decorated like an old-style gypsy wagon and features an espresso machine and coffee apparatus that would not be out of place in the highest of high-end coffee shops in all of London.

Much loved by workers in the Victoria area for being the only sniff of specialty coffee for some distance, the cart gets rightfully mobbed at lunchtimes by those far from content with the swathe of nearby chain stores. As previous winner of *Westminster Market Trader of the Year*, Flat Cap also have the accolades to go with their loyal following of satisfied customers.

LISTINGS

THE BOROUGH BARISTA

60A Seymour Street, Westminster W1H 7JN
www.theboroughbarista.com
Opening Hours: Mon-Fri: 7:30 - 5 Sat & Sun:10 - 5
Trains: Marble Arch Tube
Buses: 159, 16, 23, 36, 6, 7, 98 - Marble Arch / Edgeware Rd.

SENSORY LAB

75 Wigmore Street W1U 1QD
www.sensory-lab.co.uk
Opening Hours: Mon-Fri: 7 - 7 Sat & Sun: 10 - 5
Trains: Bond Street Tube
Buses: 113, 189, 2, 274, 30, 74, 82 - Orchard St. / Selfridges

TAYLOR ST. BARISTAS (MAYFAIR)

22 Brooks Mews, Mayfair W1K 4DY
www.taylor-st.com
Opening Hours: Mon-Fri: 8 - 5
Trains: Bond Street Tube
Buses: C2 - Berkeley Square

NOTES (COVENT GARDEN)

36 Wellington Street WC2E 7BD
www.notesmusiccoffee.com
Opening Hours: Mon-Wed: 7.30 – 9 Thurs-Fri: 7.30 – 10
Sat: 9.30 - 10 Sun: 10 - 7
Trains: Covent Garden Tube
Buses: 11, 13, 139, 15, 176, 23, 6, 87, 9 - Savoy Street

FOXCROFT & GINGER

3 Berwick Street W1F 0DR
www.foxcroftandginger.com
Opening Hours: Mon-Fri: 7 - 5 Sun: 10 - 4
Trains: Piccadilly Circus / Leicester Square Tube
Buses: 12, 159, 3, 453, 88, 94 - Conduit Street

FERNANDEZ & WELLS (ESPRESSO BAR)

16a Saint Anne's Court W1F 0BG
www.fernandezandwells.com
Opening Hours: Mon-Sat: 8 - 10
Trains: Tottenham Court Rd Tube
Buses: 25, 55, 7, 98 - Wardour Street

MONMOUTH (COVENT GARDEN)

27 Monmouth Street WC2H 9EU
www.monmouthcoffee.co.uk
Opening Hours: Mon-Sat: 8 - 6.30
Trains: Covent Garden Tube
Buses: 14, 19, 38 - Cambridge Circus

BEA'S OF BLOOMSBURY (THEOBALD'S ROAD)

44 Theobald's Road WC1X 8NW
www.beasofbloomsbury.com
Opening Hours: Mon-Fri: 8 - 7 Sat:10 - 7 Sun: 12 - 7
Trains: Chancery Lane / Holborn Tube
Buses: 19, 243, 38, 55 - Gray's Inn Road

East

The wilds of the East End have historically been synonymous with many of the grizzly tales of Old London. But far removed from the cloak and dagger stories of the past, the East has become well known as a microcosm of eclecticism, reflected in its status as the home of many of London's creative industries. These traits are also mirrored in the abundant café culture of the East, which extends from Brick Lane and Spitalfields Market, north of the river as far as Hackney Wick and the 2012 Olympic site in Stratford. The legacy of the East's industrial past also provides ideal locations and settings for some of London's foremost coffee roasters.

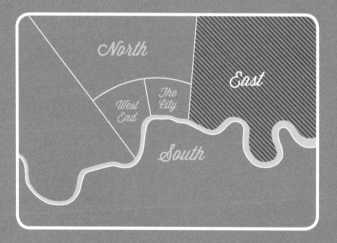

NUDE ESPRESSO

91 Brick Lane E1 6QL
T. 07804 223590
www.nudeespresso.com
Open Mon-Fri: 9 - 4   Sat: 10 - 4

On the back of over sixteen years in the coffee and hospitality trade in Australia, NZ and Canada, Nude's founders began to roast coffee from the basement of their Hanbury Street site in 2008, initially providing the espresso blends used in the café upstairs. But a year later it had become clear that their roasting operation required a dedicated space of its own, and Nude converted a stable that was once part of the nearby Truman Brewery complex, to create their very own wholesale roastery.

Tucked away from view, under an archway off Brick Lane, the unassuming exterior of the roastery with its small astroturfed seating area, hides what inside proves to be a coffee haven. Complete with cobblestone floors that sit upon the original wells and reservoirs that were used to supply water to the brewery, sacks of green coffee beans are stacked beside their 15kilo Toper drum roaster. The espresso bar here offers a more extensive range of brew methods than their café across the street, selling both their own *East* espresso blend and freshly roasted single origin coffees, making it a perfect place to brush up on your coffee knowledge whilst absorbing the inner workings of a fully-functional specialty roaster. Nude also offers one of the best deals in the city – a free coffee when you buy a bag of beans.

CLIMPSON & SONS

67 Broadway Market E8 4PH
T. 0207 254 7199
www.webshopcoffee.co.uk

East

Hours - Mon-Fri: 8 - 5
Sat: 8.30 - 5
Sun: 9.30 - 4

Trains - London Fields Rail /
Bethnal Green Tube

Buses - Routes 106,254,26,388,48,56
St. Joseph's Hospice

Loyalty Card - Yes

Wi-Fi - No

Alcohol - No

W.C. - No

Outdoor Seating - Yes

Machine - La Marzocco *Linea*

Grinders - Mazzer *Super Jolly* & *Major*, Ditting

Beans - Climpson &
Sons

The formation of East End stalwarts Climpson & Sons dates back to 2004, when founder Ian Burgess began handroasting under the name Burgil Coffee, and retailing on a Broadway Market stall. Fortuitously, this coincided not only with London's new found love affair with specialty coffee, but also with the regeneration of Broadway Market, which had begun to pave the way for independent shops and businesses in the area. Soon, Burgess' coffee stall had spawned a café, a custom roasting facility and a new name – Climpson & Sons.

Today Climpson & Sons' seasonal espresso blends and single origin coffees are not only served up by expert baristas within the Broadway Market café, they are also sold to a broad range of wholesale customers throughout London. The café has also become a prime stopping point for locals and the crowds who descend upon Broadway Market on the weekends. Burgess himself has since turned his focus to an altogether different beverage, opening the London Fields Brewery to heady acclaim in 2011.

CÀ PHÊ VN

Broadway Market E8
www.caphevn.co.uk

Hours - Sat: 10 - 5

Trains - London Fields Rail /
Bethnal Green Tube

Beans - Cà Phê VN

Buses - Routes 106,254,26,388,48,56
St. Joseph's Hospice

Vietnamese food has been a mainstay of British high street cuisine for many years now, but sadly the same cannot be said of Vietnamese coffee. One company attempting to broaden British horizons however is Cà Phê VN, a husband and wife team who met in Saigon and have since brought their love of native Vietnamese cuisine and coffee to London's East End. At their Saigon Street Café on Broadway Market, the couple serve up coffee sourced from the Dak Lak & Lam Dong regions of Vietnam, using the traditional stainless steel coffee filters, or *Phin*, to produce delicious espresso-strength brews. Their Vietnamese coffee is then either sweetened with condensed milk or used as the basis for iced coffees, also known as *ca phe da*. Besides being a welcome change to your usual coffee preference, this type of brewing can be easily transferred for use at home, providing a simple alternative to the French Press.

Such is the impact of their street café, the company now supplies coffee to Vietnamese restaurants such as the popular *Pho* chain and have since opened up another outlet on Clerkenwell Road where they can offer their renowned coffees alongside a more extensive list of food options, including their own take on the ever popular *Bánh mì*.

RAILROAD

120-122 Morning Lane, Hackney E9 6LH
T: 0208 985 2858
www.railroadhackney.co.uk

East

Hours - Mon & Tue: 10 - 5
          Wed-Sat: 10 - 11
          Sun: 10 - 5

Trains - Hackney Central/Homerton
          Overground & Rail

Buses - Routes 236, 276, 30
          Homerton Terrace

Loyalty Card - No

Wi-Fi - Yes

Alcohol - Yes

W.C. - Yes

Outdoor Seating - No

Machine - Nuova Simonelli *Aurelia*

Grinder - Anfim *Milano*

Beans - Square Mile

Having made a home in what was once a barbershop and a Nigerian wine bar, Railroad was never destined to be your average, run of the mill café. Looking part way between a traditional greasy spoon and a slick West End coffee bar, Railroad manages to strike just the right balance between classic café staples and quirky new ideas to create a very unique East London hybrid. Square Mile coffee served in handmade earthenware cups makes a welcome change from the norm, as does the menu which carries all the hallmarks of modern British gastronomy with a distinctly Asian twist, accompanied by wine and craft beers from both Kernel Brewery and Tasmania's finest, James Boag's.

From Wednesday to Saturday the café stays open for dinner in the evenings and in the basement there is a weekly open mic night featuring poetry, storytelling and live acoustic acts. The literary edge is also catered for in the small yet well stocked bookshop section of the café, featuring best-sellers, cookery books and the odd Penguin Classic thrown in for good measure.

PAVILION

Victoria Park, Crown Gate West E9 7DE
T. 0208 980 0030
www.the-pavilion-cafe.com

East

Hours - Summer: Mon-Fri: 8 - 4.30
Sat & Sun: 8 - 5
Winter: Mon-Sun: 8 - 4

Trains - Mile End /
Bethnal Green Tube

Buses - Routes 277, 425
Victoria Park

Loyalty Card - No

Wi-Fi - No

Alcohol - No

W.C. - Yes

Outdoor Seating - Yes

Machine - Synesso *Cyncra*

Grinder - Anfim *Super Caimano*

Beans - Square Mile

Park cafés are notoriously the type of outmoded British institutions which are beautifully located and yet largely underwhelming, serving up weak, instant coffee in plastic cups and food to ruin the surrounds. Seriously bucking that trend is Pavilion, housed within the beautiful glass rotunda beside the lake in Victoria Park, bringing the tradition of the park café kicking and screaming into the 21st century. Open throughout the year, Pavilion pull Square Mile's espresso blends on their Synesso and offer a pretty extensive array of hearty food options, such as full English breakfasts and bacon sandwiches - perfect warm-up fodder on those cold, wintry mornings. On sunny summer days when the tables and chairs are set out on the decking and the park is in all its glory, do expect a battle for space with the joggers and dog walkers who have unsurprisingly taken to Pavilion's contemporary slant on al fresco dining.

THE COUNTER CAFÉ

7 Roach Road E3 2PA
T. 07834 275920
www.thecountercafe.co.uk

East

Hours - Mon-Fri: 7:45 - Midnight
Sat&Sun: 9 - 1

Trains - Hackney Wick Overground/
Pudding Mill Lane DLR

Buses - Routes 276, 8, 488
Wansbeck Road

Loyalty Card - No

Wi-Fi - Yes

Alcohol - Yes

W.C. - Yes

Outdoor Seating - Yes

Machine - La Marzocco *Linea*

Grinder - Anfim *Super Caimano*

Beans - Square Mile

The Counter Café is one of London's best kept secrets and is owned and run by a brother and sister team from New Zealand, which lends the whole enterprise a healthy dose of the character and service inherent in the hospitality of their homeland. Slightly off the beaten track, nestled amongst Hackney's warehouses and workshops, the rough-around-the-edges interior, complete with battered masonry, original concrete floors, handmade furniture and rows of old cinema chairs, are indicative of the Counter's fun and unpretentious theme. Coffee comes courtesy of Square Mile, whilst on the food front the Counter serves up tapas 'til late from Thursday through Sunday. Having moved a few doors down from their original café location in 2011, the view of the new Olympic Stadium in nearby Greenwich is even more impressive than before. And for an even closer look at the Olympic village, visit the nearby Container Café – a sister project operating from a shipping container in the heart of the Olympic site.

THE HACKNEY PEARL

11 Prince Edward Road, Hackney Wick E9 5LX
T. 0208 510 3605
www.thehackneypearl.com

East

Hours - Mon-Sun: 10 - 11

Trains - Hackney Wick
Overground

Buses - Routes 26, 388, 488
Hackney Wick

Loyalty Card - Yes

Wi-Fi - Yes

Alcohol - Yes

W.C. - Yes

Outdoor Seating - Yes

Machine - Gaggia *D90 Alti*

Grinder - Mazzer *Super Jolly*

Beans - Square Mile

keep cup

Since the Hackney Pearl was crowned *Best New Café* in Time Out's 2010 Eating and Drinking Awards there has been a veritable stampede to the industrial East End and a follow-up of online reviews, which largely feature at least one jewel related pun. Aside their penchant for wordplay, they all seem to share a distinctly positive common theme: The Pearl serves up seriously good, expertly prepared food that is well worth travelling to the backstreets of Hackney to sample. Expect home made granola, bubble and squeak and sweetcorn fritters, complemented by a more substantial and ever-changing evening menu of fresh and intriguing mains. Another of the East's growing army of Square Mile affiliates, the Pearl serves up a mean coffee too.

Flying the flag for the local artist community, the Pearl has swiftly become the neighbourhood's prime meeting spot, whether sipping an espresso over breakfast or enjoying an evening taste from the list of ciders, wines, cocktails or beers from the Meantime Brewery in Greenwich.

SQUARE MILE COFFEE ROASTERS

8 Pritchard's Road E2 9AP
www.squaremilecoffee.com
By appointment only

Amid the struggle for supremacy between London's boutique coffee roasters, Square Mile is the name that has arisen as leader of innovation and forward thinking amongst the current wave of contenders. One could be forgiven for thinking that the company has been a long established name on the London coffee scene but Square Mile's meteoric ascent since they began wholesaling in 2008, has more to do with the 15 years of shared experience that its founders, James Hoffman and Annette Moldvaer, have brought to the task. By way of past credits, in 2007 they were crowned World Barista Champion and World Coffee Cup Tasting Champion respectively and have since roasted the coffees for three of the last five WBC winners.

Far from content to rest on these laurels, Square Mile's mission is to be as selective and progressive as possible, choosing only the very best new micro-lots and exciting varieties for inclusion on their wholesale list. Their seasonal espresso blends are painstakingly tweaked to represent all that the particular season conjures - be it the comforting, maple syrup sweetness of the autumn blend, to the zesty, grape acidity of their summer creation. It is this type of playfulness and ingenuity that underpins the Square Mile ethos.

Their much publicised foray into the world of pop-up coffee shops also began in 2010 in the form of the Penny University, which, for the three months it operated on Redchurch Street in Shoreditch, became one of the focal points for coffee geeks from across the globe. Boldly forsaking the usual espresso-based offerings in favour of an entirely filter coffee menu, Penny University served up an array of single origin beans prepared with chemist-like precision in syphons, drip filters and glass beakers that lined their simple wooden counter, evoking the feel of a Victorian science lab. Since then, the legacy of Penny University lives on and London has seen a heightened level of brewed coffee on café menus and a legion of baristas embracing the techniques and nuances that the variety of brew methods allows.

The impact Square Mile have had on artisanal coffee roasting in London is unsurpassed and is a testament to their hard work and commitment to quality. Unsurprisingly, Square Mile's client list currently reads like a 'who's who' of the great London coffee shops - including the likes of Prufrock, Dose, Espresso Room, Kaffeine and the Soho institution Flat White. No corner of London, it seems, is without a café serving Square Mile espresso blends or single origin beans, whilst their webshop provides coffee subscriptions, offering new and exciting micro-lots and seasonal coffees delivered directly to your door. So, until the next Square Mile experiment comes to town, there are plenty of opportunities to savour the fruits of their labour.

PRUFROCK @ PRESENT

140 Shoreditch High Street E1 6JE
www.prufrockcoffee.com
Opening Hours: Mon-Fri: 10.30 - 6 Sat: 10 - 4
Trains: Shoreditch High Street Rail & Tube
Buses: 149, 242, 26, 35, 47, 48, 67, 78 - Shoreditch

LEILA'S SHOP

17 Calvert Avenue E2 7JP
Tel: 0207 729 9789
Opening Hours: Mon-Sat: 10 - 6 Sun: 10 - 5
Trains: Old Street Tube / Shoreditch High Street Rail
Buses: 26, 48, 55 - Shoreditch Church

ALLPRESS ESPRESSO

58 Redchurch Street, Shoreditch E2 7DP
www.allpressespresso.com
Opening Hours: Mon-Fri: 8 - 5 Sat & Sun: 9 - 5
Trains: Shoreditch High Street Rail & Tube
Buses: 388, 8 - Shoreditch High Street Station

FULL STOP

202 Brick Lane E1 6SA
twitter.com/indiecoffeeuk
Opening Hours: Mon-Thurs:8-11 Fri:8-12.30 Sat:9-12.30 Sun:9-11
Trains: Shoreditch High Street Rail & Tube
Buses: 388, 8 - Brick Lane

LONG WHITE CLOUD

151 Hackney Road E2 8JL
www.longwhitecloud-hoxton.tumblr.com
Opening Hours: Mon–Fri: 7 - 7 Sat & Sun: 8 - 5
Trains: Hoxton Rail & Tube
Buses: 26, 48, 55 - Hoxton Station

REILLY ROCKET

507 Kingsland Road E8 4AU
www.reillyrocket.blogspot.com
Opening Hours: Mon–Fri: 7 - 5 Sat & Sun: 7 - 6
Trains: Dalston Junction Rail
Buses: 149, 242, 243, 488, 67, 76 - Kingsland Road/Forest Road

MOUSE & DE LOTZ

103 Shacklewell Lane E8 2EB
www.mousedelotz.com
Opening Hours: Mon & Wed-Fri: 8 - 6 Sat & Sun: 9 - 6
Trains: Dalston Kingsland Tube / Rectory Road Rail
Buses: 488 - The Petchey Academy

WILTON WAY CAFÉ

63 Wilton Way E8 1BG
www.londonfieldsradio.com
Opening Hours: Mon-Fri: 8 - 5 Sat: 8 - 6 Sun: 9 - 6
Trains: Hackney Central Rail & Tube
Buses: 242, 277, 38 - Royal Oak Road

NOMAD ESPRESSO

Netil Market, 11 - 25 Westgate Street, London Fields E8 3RL
Opening Hours: Saturday only: 11 - 6
Trains: London Fields Rail
Buses: 106, 254, 26, 388, 48, 55 - St. Joseph's Hospice

ANDOR BUREAU

3 Mare Street, Hackney E8 4RP
www.andorbureau.com
Opening Hours: Mon-Fri: 7 - 7 Sat & Sun: 9 - 7
Trains: Cambridge Heath Rail
Buses: 106, 254, 26, 388, 48, 55 - Mare Street

HURWUNDEKI

299 Railway Arches, Cambridge Heath Road E2 9HA
www.hurwundeki.com
Opening Hours: Mon-Fri: 7 - 6. Sat & Sun: 9 - 6
Trains: Cambridge Heath Rail
Buses: 106, 254, 388, D6 - Cambridge Heath Station

TAYLOR ST. BARISTAS (CANARY WHARF)

8 South Colonnade, Canary Wharf E14 4PZ
www.taylor-st.com
Opening Hours: See Website
Trains: Canary Wharf DLR
Buses: 135, 277, D3, D7, D8 - Canary Wharf Station

CONTAINER CAFÉ

The View Tube, The Greenway, Marshgate Lane E15 2PT
www.theviewtube.co.uk
Opening Hours: Mon-Fri: 9 - 5 Sat & Sun: 10 - 6
Trains: Pudding Mill Lane DLR / Stratford Tube
Buses: 108, 25, 276, 339, 425 - Abbey Lane

GRIND COFFEE BAR

The Great Eastern Market, Westfield Stratford City E20
www.grindcoffeebar.co.uk
Opening Hours: Mon-Fri:10 - 9 Sat: 9 - 9 Sun: 11 - 5
Trains: Stratford Tube / Stratford DLR
Buses: 241, 339, 97 - Stratford City Bus Station

Recieve a 20% discount from
1 November 2011 – 31 January 2012

Use promo code: VESPERTINE to receive the
discount on all online purchases at keepcup.com

North

The North of London is a term applied to a vast area spreading from Islington at its southern-most point to the borough of Enfield in its Northern extremity. Covering such a large area of the city, the North contains a diverse range of communities, each with their own attractions and individual appeal. Specialty coffee has found its place within these pockets of Greater London, though with nowhere near the prevalence as the capital's more central areas. However, little neighbourhood gems have appeared in recent years, providing the local communities with their very own specialty coffee haunts. Furthermore, it is only a matter of time before London's growing taste for quality coffee sees the proliferation of cafés and community hubs extend to all reaches of the area.

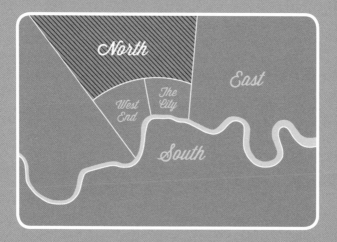

TINA, WE SALUTE YOU

47 King Henry's Walk, Islington N1 4NH
T. 0203 119 0047
www.tinawesaluteyou.com

North

Hours - Tue-Fri: 8 - 8
Sat & Sun: 10 - 7

Trains - Dalston Kingsland
Overground

Buses - Routes 67, 76, 149, 243, 488
Dalston Kingsland Station

Loyalty Card - Yes

Wi-Fi - Yes

Alcohol - No

W.C. - Yes

Outdoor Seating - Yes

Machine - La Marzocco *Linea*

Grinders - Anfim *Milano* & Mazzer *Luigi*

Beans - Square Mile

D anny Hilton and Steve Hawkes used to run a market stall near Brick Lane selling cupcakes, upon which their copy of J.H. Lynch's painting *Tina*, took pride of place. When they decided to upscale and set up their very own coffee shop in 2009, both the delicious cakes and their prized ornament came with them and Tina, We Salute You was born.

The walls of the café serve as a blank canvas for East London's finest illustrators, designers and painters whilst also serving as an impromptu loyalty system, whereby regulars can keep track of their coffee tally with marker pens. Besides the charming name, the ever-changing scenery and a locale which has been described as "the coolest place in Britain" by various parts of the media, Tina's has yet another ace up its sleeve – you won't find a better cup of coffee anywhere in Dalston. On busy days expect to find chairs skirting the pavement outside and a collection of fashionistas doing their best to live up to the area's stylish reputation. After all, Tina's is the place to be, and with good reason.

GINGER & WHITE

4a-5a St. Perrins Court, Hampstead NW3 1QS
T. 0207 431 9098
www.gingerandwhite.com

Hours - Mon-Fri: 7.30 - 5.30
        Sat & Sun: 8.30 - 5.30

Trains - Hampstead Rail

Buses - Routes 46, 268
        Hampstead High Street

Loyalty Card - Yes

Wi-Fi - Yes

Alcohol - No

W.C. - Yes

Outdoor Seating - Yes

Machine - La Marzocco *Linea*

Grinders - Mazzer *Robur E*, Anfim *Super Caimano*,
           Mahlkönig *Tanzania*

Beans - Square Mile

A short stroll from John Keats's opulent former residence will find you at the doorstep of yet another of Hampstead's must visit locations. Ginger & White models itself as a quintessentially British coffee shop and its design and menu carry pleasant hallmarks of the nation's contemporary culinary tradition. With reclaimed furniture and comfortable nooks, alongside plenty of Union Jack imagery, this is a place to experience the finer things in life, including coffee that thankfully far exceeds the lowly standards the U.K. has been known for previously. Alongside the beverages, the breakfast and brunch food is as delicious as it is eccentric, featuring porridge, pastries, granola and, perhaps most notably, boiled eggs with their own knitted bobble hats. Add to this baristas and waiting staff who are hugely efficient and friendly, with owners who have their finger on the pulse of London's coffee scene and Ginger & White adds up to the kind of place that makes you justifiably proud to be British.

FRED & FRAN

55 Kynaston Road, Stoke Newington N16 0EB
T. 07788 158742
www.fredandfran.com

Hours - Mon-Fri: 8 - 5 (Tue: closed)
        Sat: 9 - 5
        Sun: 9 - 4

Trains - Stoke Newington Rail

Buses - Routes 393, 476, 73
        Bouverie Road

Loyalty Card - No

Wi-Fi - Yes

Alcohol - No

W.C. - Yes

Outdoor Seating - Yes

Machine - La Marzocco *Linea*

Grinders - Mazzer *Super Jolly*, Anfim *Super Caimano*

Beans - Square Mile

For some time Stoke Newington had been bereft of a coffee-focussed venue to call its own, despite playing host to countless cafés and residents that were calling out for good coffee. That is until September 2011, when Fred & Fran arrived to fill that ample void.

Named after her grandparents, owner Demelza Donohoo set up the café having previously supplied her magnificent home-made cakes to coffee shops such as Flat White and Wilton Way. With her fresh-from-the-oven produce now permanently parked on the counter top, Square Mile coffee in the hopper and a small but beautiful patio area out back, Fred & Fran is already being recognised as the area's premier niche by Stokie locals who have long been starved of such simple pleasures. In time, as the influence of specialty coffee becomes more widespread, the area will no doubt have many more cafés looking to follow Demelza's lead.

MERITO COFFEE

Eton Avenue, Swiss Cottage NW3
www.meritocoffee.com

Hours - Wed & Fri: 8.30 - 3

Trains - Swiss Cottage Tube

Buses - Routes 113,13,187,268,82
Swiss Cottage Station

Machine - Izzo

Grinders - Mazzer *Super Jolly*,
La Minerva

Beans - Coffee Plant

The Swiss Cottage tube station has five exits. Follow exits 1, 3, 4 and 5 and you will experience particularly barren coffee country. But follow exit 2 and you'll ascend to an unexpected coffee oasis in the form of the Merito Coffee stall.

Merito has been Swiss Cottage Market's saving grace for over seven years now and has gathered an exceptionally loyal customer base who often stop by for an entertaining chat. Merito's owner Jason Fitzpatrick believes that good coffee speaks for itself and is weary of evangelizing. He is, however, very knowledgeable and always willing to help guide customers' tastes. With beans roasted by Coffee Plant in Notting Hill and blended by Jason himself, Merito is one of the few carts that serves both espresso-based drinks and filter coffee from their hand-fashioned pour over bar. Although only open on Wednesdays and Fridays at their Swiss Cottage pitch, on Saturdays you can also find them serving up great coffee on Broadway Market, Hackney.

Alike the East of the city, London's southern districts now play host to a number of prominent artisanal coffee roasters who have set about single-handedly transforming the once fallow coffee territory into a fertile ground for independent cafés. Whilst the South has a less glamorous image than other areas of London, its suburbs have since become the latest section of the city to embrace the rise of specialty coffee. Denoting a huge area south of the river, which extends to the Northern-most reaches of Surrey, expect the south to flourish in the coming years as the strength of their already impressive list of coffee shops and roasters grows ever stronger and more diverse.

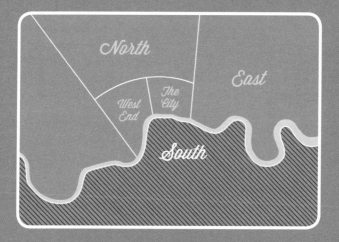

MONMOUTH COFFEE

34 Maltby Street, Bermondsey SE1 3PA
T. 0207 232 3010
www.monmouthcoffee.co.uk
Open Saturday: 9am to 2pm

Inspired by the way in which organic and whole food companies had begun to source and trade their produce, Monmouth founder Anita Le Roy embarked upon her own personal exploration of buying and roasting green coffee back in 1978. The idea was to emulate the clarity and transparency that her contemporaries at the newly established Neal's Yard brought to their business, in order to both revolutionise the industry and bring an altogether higher quality of coffee to London's consumers.

Though the journey was at times perilous, when Monmouth first opened its doors in Covent Garden three decades ago, few could have predicted that Le Roy's vision would go on to enkindle the enthusiasm of a multitude of coffee drinkers, cafés and roasters, or that Monmouth's tenure at the summit of specialty coffee would have endured for so long.

With an old fashioned UNO roaster in the basement and a shop selling the roasted beans up top, this primary venue was a homage to coffee retail, offering an exclusively filter-based coffee menu to highlight the different characteristics of the varietals on sale.

In 2007, the company moved their roastery from the basement in Covent Garden to their current Bermondsey home, where they have upgraded from their severely fatigued 1930s Whitmee which had carried the burden of the high level operation for many years. Now, under the railway arches of their impressive Maltby Street site, two Petroncini roasters - one 60 kilo and the other 20 kilo - churn out a staggering four tonnes of roasted coffee every week. A percentage of the coffee roasted goes to wholesale customers throughout the country, whilst the majority of the beans are still sold over the counters at Monmouth Borough Market and the perennial Covent Garden site, where the aim is to provide customers with a choice of flavour profiles and to introduce carefully selected new coffees and micro-lots throughout the year.

You could call Monmouth the grand old lady of London coffee, only that such a moniker fails to conjure the forward thinking, egalitarian spirit that pervades their methods. Whilst superficially little seems to have changed during its thirty year life-span to date, Monmouth continues to promote ethical trade and to plough altogether new furrows. As it was in the late seventies, they are still heavily invested in a transparent supply chain from growers and co-operatives, where the farmer sets the initial price of their crop. Last year the company also began buying green coffee directly from origin for the first time. In essence, Monmouth defines much of what is good about London's flourishing coffee business, employing the same classic branding, an emphasis on better practice and an insistence on equal and sustainable trade, to constantly reinvent their time-honoured tradition of near perfect results.

BROWNS OF BROCKLEY

5-6 Coulgate Street SE4 2RW
twitter.com/brownsofse4

Hours - Mon-Thurs: 7 -11, Fri: 7 - 5
Sat: 9 - 5, Sun: 9 - 3

Trains - Brockley Overground & Rail

Buses - Routes 171, 172, 484
Brockley Station

Loyalty Card - Yes

Wi-Fi - Yes

Alcohol - Yes

W.C. - Yes

Outdoor Seating - No

Machine - La Marzocco *FB/70*

Grinder - Anfim *Super Caimano*

Beans - Square Mile

Brockley may seem an unlikely place to find some of the best coffee south of the river, but Browns of Brockley's presence in the South London suburb has been a catalyst in the formation of a flourishing coffee community there. Away from the clamour of the city centre, Browns is a laid back antidote for all those commuting each day on the London Overground line just across the street. Owner Ross Brown set up shop in 2009 having spent time in the U.S. honing his barista skills and both he and his colleagues were entrants in the U.K. Brewers Cup in 2011. Alongside dutifully prepared coffee, the food options include jaw defying sandwiches and a range of freshly made snacks and salads. Everyone involved with the café is as affable and friendly as Browns of Brockley's official mascot, Ludd the pug, whose image adorns the walls, menus and loyalty cards. The café also becomes a hive of activity on the weekends when the community comes out in force for the nearby Brockley Market.

No.5 COLLGATE STREET, SE4 2RW 020 8692 0722

DARK FLUID

Brockley Market, Lewisham College Car Park
Lewisham Way SE4 1UT
www.darkfluid.co.uk

Hours - Sat: 10 - 2

Trains - St. John's Rail

Buses - Routes 136, 21, 321, 436
Lewisham College

Machine - Kees van der Westen
Mirage
Grinders - Mazzer *Robur E*,
Grindmaster *800*
Beans - Dark Fluid

Whilst working as a chef in Michelin Star restaurants, Dark Fluid's main man Lawrence Sinclair became interested in applying the same meticulous care to the preparation and provenance of coffee as the gourmet ingredients he used in his profession. After some successful experiments using a paint stripping heat gun and a bag of Kenyan AA, Lawrence discovered a small 300g Hottop drum roaster and his interest and passion for coffee spilled over into full-blown obsession.

In 2007, Lawrence found an outlet for his homespun expertise, joining forces with former U.K. latte art champion Neil le Bihan on his Exchange Coffee stall. In 2011 their hard graft was to pay dividends when the duo raised eyebrows by being placed 2nd in the U.K. Barista Championships using coffee that Lawrence had roasted in a converted shed in Lewisham. Having caused a stir amongst London's coffee glitterati, Lawrence has since set up his own roastery, using a heavily modified Turkish drum roaster to create espresso blends and unique single origins for select local cafés and his Dark Fluid coffee stall at Brockley Market. With a fresh and inventive approach, businesses like Dark Fluid are becoming integral to coffee's growing suburban outreach.

FEDERATION COFFEE

46 Granville Arcade, Brixton Village Market
Coldharbour Lane SW9 8PS
www.federationcoffee.com

South

Hours - Mon-Fri: 8 - 5
Sat: 9.30 - 5

Trains - Brixton Tube

Buses - Routes - 322, 3, 35, 355, 59, 2
Brixton Station

Loyalty Card - Yes

Wi-Fi - Yes

Alcohol - No

W.C. - No

Outdoor Seating - N/A

Machine - La Marzocco *Linea*

Grinders - Mazzer *Robur E*, Mahlkönig *Vario*

Alternative Brewing Methods - Pour Over

Beans - Federation
Nude Espresso

When Federation opened in Brixton back in 2010, the Village Market had seen better days. The boarded units and lack of passing trade were a far cry from the market of old, that had once been one of Brixton's cultural landmarks. But recently a regeneration of the market has occurred, thanks in no small part to independent food companies and traders like Federation, who have made their homes under its vaulted ceilings.

Federation was founded by Kiwis Nick Coates and George Wallace, who sacrificed their careers in London's financial sector to follow their shared dream of working in coffee. They have recently completed Federation's very own roasting facility in a nearby warehouse, which has begun to supply the café with freshly roasted origins and blends. Having consistently served the best coffee in Brixton for some time, Federation are now revelling in their newly invigorated surrounds. Don't expect the market's revival to end there.

GRIND COFFEE BAR

79 Lower Richmond Road SW15 2QJ
T. 0208 789 5101
www.grindcoffeebar.co.uk

South

Hours - Mon-Fri: 7.30 - 4 Sat&Sun: 8.30 - 5	Loyalty Card - No
	Wi-Fi - Yes
Trains - Putney Bridge Tube / Putney High Street Rail	Alcohol - No
	W.C. - Yes
Buses - Route 265, 22, 485 Ruvigny Gardens	Outdoor Seating - Yes

Machine - La Marzocco *Strada EP*   Beans - London Roasters

Grinders - Anfim *Super Caimano*, Mazzer *Super Jolly*

Considering the ample number of Antipodean ex-pats living within the SW area code, it's a wonder it took so long for Putney to have a coffee shop worthy of those in the southern hemisphere. Upon such un-mined ground for speciality coffee, Grind Coffee Bar has flourished since arriving in 2010 and has rapidly arisen as one of the premier coffee spots in the south. Having fast outgrown the confines of the music shop in which the first Grind concession was located, the much larger site, which is a short stroll along the river West of Putney Bridge, has itself already engendered yet another café in Stratford's new Westfield shopping centre, adjacent to the 2012 Olympic village. The fundamental recipe for their success? An espresso blend from London Roasters pulled on a gleaming La Marzocco by skilled, experienced baristas. What more could a caffeine starved London suburbanite ask for?

VOLCANO COFFEE WORKS

**Unit D17, Parkhall Trading Estate
62 Tritton Road SE21 8DE
T. 0208 761 8415
www.volcanocoffeeworks.com**
By appointment only

Kurt Stewart visited the U.K. from his native New Zealand in 1994 with the intention of staying for six weeks. However, over a decade that has involved him chefing, home roasting, running a coffee cart the length and breadth of south London and then establishing Volcano Coffee Works in 2009, Kurt has never looked back.

As a lover of mechanics with a history of refurbishing scooters and old lever pull espresso machines, it's no wonder that Kurt's roastery has the feel of an engineering workshop, with its fair share of build projects on the work benches and his Piaggio *Ape* coffee cart parked under the hand-built mezzanine. Housed within what was once the old Pye Electronics factory, the roastery features a somewhat unknown Mexican *Maqafe* roaster, renovated by Kurt himself, which is now used to roast Volcano's seasonal espresso - a full to medium blend which, by London's standards, teeters on the cusp of darkness. For now Volcano coffee is mostly served in nearby concessions, though there are plans afoot to adapt a part of the original factory to accommodate Volcano's very own coffee shop, which should in turn help caffeinate the group of potters, glass blowers and artisans who share the building. Watch this space...

MONMOUTH COFFEE (BOROUGH MARKET)

2 Park Street, The Borough SE1 9AB
www.monmouthcoffee.co.uk
Opening Hours: Mon-Fri: 7.30 - 6
Trains: London Bridge / Borough Tube
Buses: 381, RV1 - The Hop Exchange

FLAT CAP COFFEE CO. (BOROUGH MARKET)

Borough Market SE1 1TL
www.notesmusiccoffee.com
Opening Hours: Thurs: 11 - 5 Fri: 12 - 6 Sat: 8 - 5
Trains: London Bridge / Borough Tube
Buses: 381, RV1 - The Hop Exchange

SCOOTERCAFFÈ

132 Lower Marsh, Lambeth SE1 7AE
Tel: 0207 620 1421
Opening Hours: Mon-Thurs: 8.30 - 1 Fri: 8.30 - 12 Sat: 10 - 12
Trains: Lambeth North / Waterloo Tube
Buses: 12, 148, 159, 341, 453, 53, 76 - Lower Marsh

THE ROASTERY

789 Wandsworth Road SW8 3JQ
twitter.com/TheRoastery
Opening Hours: Mon-Fri: 7.30 - 3.30 Sat & Sun: 9 - 3.30
Trains: Wandsworth Road Rail / Clapham Common Tube
Buses: 452, 77, 87 - Victoria Rise

FEDERATION COFFEE 2.0

9 Brighton Terrace, Brixton SW9 8DJ
www.federationcoffee.com
Opening Hours: Mon-Fri: 8 - 4
Trains: Brixton Rail / Tube
Buses: 322, 3, 35, 355, 59, 2 - Brixton Station

ST. DAVID COFFEE HOUSE

5 David's Road, Forest Hill SE23 3EP
www.stdavidcoffeehouse.co.uk
Opening Hours: Tue-Fri: 8 - 6 Sat: 9 - 5 Sun: 9.30 - 4
Trains: Forest Hill Rail
Buses: 176, 197 - Forest Hill Station / London Road

YOU DON'T BRING ME FLOWERS

15 Staplehurst Road SE13 5ND
www.youdontbringmeflowers.co.uk
Opening Hours: Tues-Fri: 8 - 6 Sat: 9 - 6 Sun: 10 - 5
Trains: Hither Green Rail
Buses: 225 - Hither Green Station

THE LONDON PARTICULAR

399 New Cross Road SE14 6LA
www.thelondonparticular.co.uk
Opening Hours: Mon-Fri: 7.30 - 5 Sat: 10 - 4
Trains: New Cross Rail
Buses: 177, 225, 453, 53 - New Cross Station

TAYLOR ST. BARISTAS (RICHMOND)

Unit 3, Westminster House, Richmond TW9 2ND
www.taylor-st.com
Opening Hours: Mon-Fri: 7.30 - 5 Sat: 9 - 5
Trains: Richmond Rail
Buses: 371, 493, 65 - Richmond Station

CoffeeHit

...The place to get all your coffee gear

Coffee Compendium

Coffea Arabica

A HISTORY OF
LONDON COFFEE HOUSES

The history of the humble coffee plant spans well over a thousand years and is as dark and as complex as the brew itself. From its origins in the Horn of Africa to the billion dollar industry it has engendered, coffee has endured a tumultuous and remarkable passage, viewed at various points in its history as both the drink of the masses and as the luxury of Kings; a gift of the Gods and, conversely, a sin by which one could lose one's soul to the Devil. By the time it had arrived on English soil, having travelled from Ethiopia to the Arabian Peninsula via the ancient ports of Mocha and Jidda, before finding its way into Europe and the Mediterranean, coffee had already become an intrinsic part of societal ritual in many parts of the globe, with a legacy of dedicated drinking venues prompted by the first known coffee house, which opened in Constantinople in 1554.

London's premier coffee house began trading on St. Michael's Alley, Cornhill in 1652. Established by Pasqua Rosée, a Greek or Armenian servant to a wealthy English merchant named Daniel Edwards, this seminal London coffee house proved extremely popular, if not for the exotic ritual afforded the drink then for the host of medicinal properties Rosée ascribed it. In a handbill entitled *The Vertue of the Coffee Drink*, that is displayed in the British Museum, Rosée claimed that coffee could cure gout, scurvy, dropsy, ailments of the lungs and even miscarriages. In line with its perceived medicinal qualities, which were also curiously embellished by some medical professionals, the drink was initially consumed as more of a medicament than a tasty beverage, used to enliven the senses and even provide a safer alternative to opium addiction. Due to poor sanitation and unclean drinking water, a boiled beverage like coffee also became a preferable substitute to wine and ale, whose negative, soporific effects – such as public drunkenness and stomach ailments - were already extremely prevalent in 17th century England.

Accounts of how coffee was prepared and served in these early coffee shops are scarce, though it is reported that coffee was most commonly taken black, without sugar or sweeteners. Coffee roasting would have either taken place in the coffee houses themselves or in premises akin to early coffee roasteries, where beans were roasted over charcoal fires, either in pans or turned on spits using primitive devices such as cylinder roasters, which appeared in London around 1660. Before the advent of coffee mills and grinders, the roasted beans would have then been ground or 'garbled' in a mortar before brewing.

In December 1660, Samuel Pepys made note of Rosée's coffee house, writing *"the first time that ever I was there, and I found much pleasure in it"*. Indeed, the notoriety that Rosée's venture generated soon became widespread and coffee houses rapidly proliferated.

GARRAWAY'S COFFEE-HOUSE. *(From a sketch taken shortly before its demolition)*

Borrowing from the traditions of the coffee houses of the Middle East, which had become known as patriarchal social hubs where men met to drink coffee, play chess, make music and to sing, London's first historical coffee houses were abundant with exotic references. Many sold tobacco products, chocolate and tea whilst others provided hookah pipes for customers' use. Signs outside these establishments often depicted middle-eastern imagery and some even had foreign staff or servants to provide a spectacle and authenticity to the surrounds. With names such as the *Turk's Head*, *Jerusalem Coffee House*, *Morat Ye Great* and the *Oriental Cigar Divan*, these early coffee shops not only satisfied Britain's cultural fascination with the East during the Georgian period, they also fast became as ubiquitous and populated as those in the Muslim world.

London's coffee houses were often large, simply furnished rooms with communal tables that became renowned hotbeds of lively conjecture and debate. The tendency for their patrons' discourse was to provoke the nickname *penny universities* – so applied because, for the entry fee of a penny, the average layman had access not only to coffee but also to the education afforded by newspapers, pamphlets, discussion and gossip. At a time when the postal service was disorganised, coffee houses also served as stopping points for agents to circulate and impart up-to-the-minute renditions of the city's news. Along with the supporting role coffee houses played in the distribution of London's news and print culture, there were distinct venues for different industries and persuasions. For example, *Garraway's* on Exchange Alley was rife with merchant trade and the London Stock Exchange began life as a coffee house called *Jonathan's*, where its owner would put up commodity prices on the wall for his stock-trader clientele. In 1668, *Lloyd's Coffee House* opened on Tower Street and was to spawn what is today one of the most famous insurance companies in the world. Similarly, *Nando's Coffee House*, one of the few structural survivors which stands at the Western End of Fleet Street, became the habitué of members of the legal fraternity and so became known colloquially as 'the bar by the bar'.

Neither the Great Fire of 1666, which decimated large portions of London's overcrowded, timber-built habitation, nor the Plague which took the lives of an estimated twenty percent of the city's population the previous year, could halt the spread of coffee houses. Those destroyed were mostly rehoused or rebuilt, funded by their ardent and often wealthy patrons, and those that ceased trading as a consequence did little to prevent altogether new coffee shops from opening. The public's growing appreciation for coffee houses was summed up in 1673, when an anonymous author wrote:

"A coffee house is a lay conventicle, good fellowship turned puritan...whither people come, after toping all day, to purchase at the expense of their last penny, the repute of sober companions."

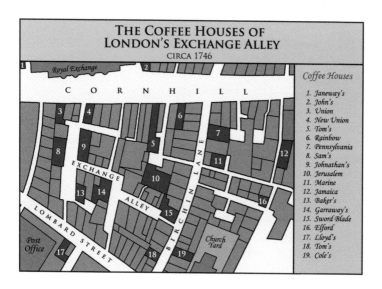

THE COFFEE HOUSES OF LONDON'S EXCHANGE ALLEY
CIRCA 1746

Coffee Houses

1. Janeway's
2. John's
3. Union
4. New Union
5. Tom's
6. Rainbow
7. Pennsylvania
8. Sam's
9. Johnathan's
10. Jerusalem
11. Marine
12. Jamaica
13. Baker's
14. Garraway's
15. Sword Blade
16. Elford
17. Lloyd's
18. Tom's
19. Cole's

However, other sections of the community where less than supportive of London's new-found pastime. In response to the adulation afforded coffee houses and perhaps, in part, their exclusion from them, the *Women's Petition Against Coffee* was circulated in 1674, which bemoaned their spouse's partaking in 'the excessive use of this drying enfeebling Liquor'. Furthermore, in December 1675, King Charles II responded angrily to the free and potentially treasonous speech that was commonplace within the coffee houses, branding them "seminaries of sedition" and ordering their closure. But the King's proclamation caused uproar within the city, not only from the general public but likewise from royal aides and associates, who advised the King to withdraw his directive. After just eleven days, Charles conceded and lifted the ban, though not before imposing a new taxation of coffee and outlawing the distribution of pamphlets or books within the coffee houses. In retrospect, the King's short-lived prohibition not only increased anti-royalist sentiment but also heightened the popularity of the coffee house; by 1715 they numbered over two thousand in London alone.

The coffee house's propensity for harbouring creativity and radical thinking appears to be a recurring theme throughout history. Certainly, much of the romance and poetical eulogizing they are afforded stems from the literary figures, philosophers and characters who sought refuge within them. Whilst not dissimilar in style to alehouses, coffee houses encouraged sobriety and cogent conversation, and drew personalities whom provided rich material for authors and playwrights short of a character or two. *The Sultaness Coffee House*, attributed with being the first in London to serve tea, is also notable for being featured in several of Charles Dickens's works, whilst others such as *Will's* in Covent Garden attracted a crowd of London literati, often referred to as 'The Wits'. Famous authors such as John Dryden, Jonathan Swift and Alexander Pope all frequented West End coffee houses, where satirical verse and heated high-brow hearsay were renowned. By the late 17th century, coffee shops also began to open their doors in other European capital cities such as Paris, Vienna and Hamburg, where they became similarly famous as the offices and hangouts for a host of prominent social figures.

By 1750, coffee was being grown on five continents and its cultivation and export had become a multimillion-pound enterprise. But as coffee and its ritual habitats spread to all four corners of the world, the popularity of coffee houses and coffee drinking in London began to decline. Having been first sold in the coffee houses of London, tea's favour had gradually risen due to influential advertising campaigns by tea's primary importer, the East India Company, and endorsement from the upper classes. This was to prove fortuitous as, following the 1870s epidemic of coffee rust – a lethal fungus that renders the coffee plant unusable – Britain was able to supplant their coffee growing operations in Sri Lanka and India with tea instead. Tea and coffee had also begun being consumed in homes and, unlike coffee, tea required no roasting, grinding and brewing, simply hot water. Exclusive clubs for the social elite had also become popular, starving the coffee shops of their previous custom. All this conspired against coffee's popularity and by the early 19th century, few coffee houses remained in London and many were converted to alehouses or else stopped trading altogether. Whilst coffee continued its tour of the world and was becoming interwoven with the customs of different cities and nations, London's coffee houses had vanished almost as rapidly as they had arisen. It would be several centuries before the fervour surrounding coffee's introduction to London would be rekindled once more.

With the advent of new technologies, the 20th Century marked the birth of a new espresso culture in London when the first *Gaggia* machine was imported in 1952. By 1956 there were over four hundred cafés inspired by the cosmopolitan coffee culture enjoyed by our Italian counterparts. However, it is only in recent years that cafés in the UK have begun to reflect the speciality coffee movement seen in Australia, New Zealand and some parts of the US. Driven by a new breed of independent, specialty roasters and cafés, London now has one of the greatest coffee scenes in the world with a vitality unparalleled since coffee's arrival in the city some three hundred years ago.

WORLDWIDE COFFEE PRODUCTION

The map below illustrates the largest coffee producing nations worldwide. They consist of some of the world's poorest counties and production is confined to regions no more than one thousand miles from the equator.

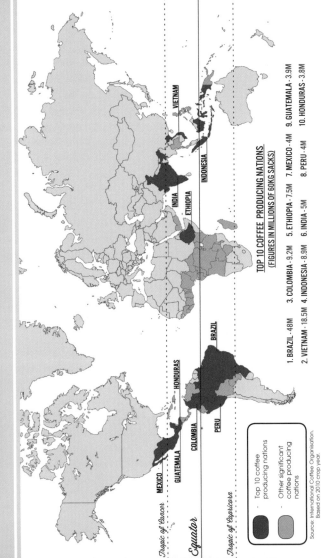

TOP 10 COFFEE PRODUCING NATIONS
(FIGURES IN MILLIONS OF 60KG SACKS)

1. BRAZIL - 48M
2. VIETNAM - 18.5M
3. COLOMBIA - 9.2M
4. INDONESIA - 8.9M
5. ETHIOPIA - 7.5M
6. INDIA - 5M
7. MEXICO - 4M
8. PERU - 4M
9. GUATEMALA - 3.9M
10. HONDURAS - 3.8M

- Top 10 coffee producing nations
- Other significant coffee producing nations

Source: International Coffee Organisation.
Based on 2010 crop year.

WORLDWIDE COFFEE CONSUMPTION

This map depicts the nations with the highest levels of coffee consumption per capita, per year. As you can see, the largest consumers are concentrated in the comparatively wealthy European nations, directly contrasting the map above.

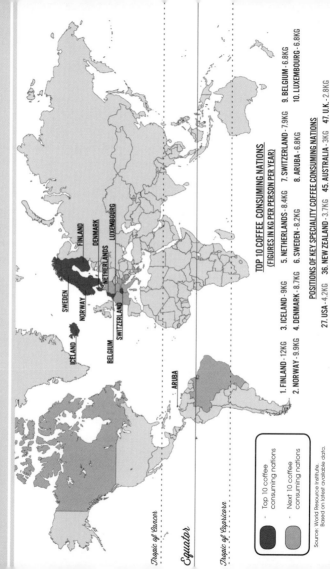

TOP 10 COFFEE CONSUMING NATIONS
(FIGURES IN KG PER PERSON PER YEAR)

1. FINLAND - 12KG
2. NORWAY - 9.9KG
3. ICELAND - 9KG
4. DENMARK - 8.7KG
5. NETHERLANDS - 8.4KG
6. SWEDEN - 8.2KG
7. SWITZERLAND - 7.9KG
8. ARUBA - 6.8KG
9. BELGIUM - 6.8KG
10. LUXEMBOURG - 6.8KG

POSITIONS OF KEY SPECIALITY COFFEE CONSUMING NATIONS

27. USA - 4.2KG   36. NEW ZEALAND - 3.7KG   45. AUSTRALIA - 3KG   47. U.K. - 2.8KG

Map labels: ICELAND, NORWAY, SWEDEN, FINLAND, DENMARK, NETHERLANDS, LUXEMBOURG, BELGIUM, SWITZERLAND, ARUBA

Tropic of Cancer
Equator
Tropic of Capricorn

Legend:
- Top 10 coffee consuming nations
- Next 10 coffee consuming nations

Source: World Resource Institute.
Based on latest available data.

THE ETHICS OF COFFEE BUYING

By Steven Macatonia
UNION HAND-ROASTED COFFEE

Our ethos at Union Hand-Roasted Coffee is to craft a superior coffee experience, driven by an insistence on buying high quality coffee and engaging with expert coffee farmers with whom we are proud to trade. As coffee buyer for Union, it is also my primary challenge and concern to source our coffee responsibly and to ensure it is authentically produced in a sustainable and ethical environment. But despite a growing interest from consumers and coffee enthusiasts, the complexities of this crucial selection process are generally misunderstood. Where Fairtrade's intentions and programmes are clearly defined, it remains obscured by the intricacies of its deployment, as well as its actual content. Direct Trade is a system devised to challenge the difficulties arising in how coffee is commonly traded and is an approach that can transform a standard partnership into a long-term direct trade relationship. However, coffee sourcing and buying is an intricate and hazard-fraught process, whatever system of buying is employed, and presents many challenges that one may not ordinarily consider.

Over a period of 15 years, Jeremy and I have experienced first-hand the temperaments, fluctuations and disparities affecting the coffee industry, buying coffee in every way imaginable. Broadly speaking, these methods fall into two distinct categories. The most traditional method, called 'Spot Market' coffee buying, masks the producer as well as the price they receive, furthermore ignoring the issues relating to its origin. The other common method is to buy coffee contracted through an importer, where 'lots' can be Fairtrade certified and may include transparent provenance and contact with the grower, but with a limited influence to work directly with them or to enhance the quality of their coffee via incentive premiums. Through trial and error, we have found that neither Spot Market trade or buying via importers meets our long term aspirations, either in terms of communication and interaction with farmers or sourcing the level of quality we demand.

Fairtrade can represent an effective economic model by offering a minimum price that constitutes a 'safety-net', shielding small-scale farmers from economic hardships when the market plummets. However, specialty grade coffee is traded on the intrinsic values of its quality and taste profiles, features that significantly surpass commodity grade coffee as well as the Fairtrade standard. From our experience, buying Fairtrade coffee alone does not encourage innovation - its primary objectives are rather directed towards encouraging the establishment of particular work structures, health and safety regulations, in addition to meeting sustainable development goals.

At Union, we feel limited by what the Fairtrade certification could achieve for the farmers we buy from, particularly with regards to the quality of the coffee. Therefore, we evolved our coffee buying philosophy to go beyond Fairtrade, which we call Union Direct Trade. Our definition of Direct Trade is an open contact and price transparency along with a free dialogue leading to long-term relationships, which assist in achieving improvements in quality.

Essentially, Union Direct Trade benefits both ourselves, coffee farmers and also the coffee consumer. For us it means we are not restricted by being limited to Fairtrade, giving access to a diverse range of high quality, ethically sourced coffees and to evaluate first-hand provenance of the circumstances of producers at origin. It also creates a foundation for our personal relationships with farmers, essential for timely knowledge about quality as well as social and environmental concerns. Furthermore, it enables Union to communicate the stories of coffee producers with authenticity.

The Direct Trade approach eliminates the 'middlemen' or coyotes who buy in the local market and also the traditional export and import agents which enables farmers free negotiation on price and opens up transparent costs throughout the supply chain. It establishes a baseline price with premiums for quality, rewarding farmers who innovate and improve the value of their crop and supports forward financing for small-scale farmers most in need.

Coffee enthusiasts who are seeking ethically produced, high quality coffee need to ask probing questions to gather detailed information about the ethos of coffee sourcing. Union Direct Trade allows customers peace of mind when choosing any of the coffees we have sourced and roasted, whilst ensuring that the quality of coffee in your cup promotes the best seasonal lots and coffees it is possible to find.

Undertaking our Direct Trade program requires getting our boots dirty and making frequent origin visits for direct face-to-face meetings with producers. This is necessary to plan strategy for the coming seasons and to review and enjoy successful achievements. We believe this is the most effective way to expand economic opportunity and for small scale farmers to earn a sustainable livelihood by producing high quality coffee. In our experience Union Direct Trade is the model that allows all participants in the supply chain to gain a fuller experience of the complex world of coffee and an appreciation for the environment in which it is produced and enjoyed.

Women in a Coffee Kids-supported organic gardening project in Oaxaca, Mexico, show off the fruits of their labor.

COFFEE KIDS

Sustainable, high-quality coffee can only come from sustainable, healthy communities. For the past 23 years, Coffee Kids has brought change to coffee-producing communities.

Help us bring prosperity full circle.

www.coffeekids.org

COFFEE ROASTING
By Lawrence Sinclair
DARK FLUID

Coffee roasting has two sides, a split personality if you like. There is a romantic side filled with beautiful imagery of 1950s cast iron machinery, pale blue flames, jute sacks and flowing trays of roasted beans. But behind the romance is a world of logistics, order, record keeping and tasting... lots of tasting. For those who care to look, coffee is an enormous and diverse subject, with a plethora of producing countries, types of bean and grades of quality. Coffee roasting holds all the wonder, fascination and challenges of restaurant cooking and the desire to find and roast the best coffee in the world can become an obsession.

Half the challenge of roasting coffee is sourcing the beans. Some, not all, hold the potential for beautiful roasted coffee - all we have to do is find those beans. Essentially, the better green coffee, the better the brewed coffee. The way they are produced, graded and processed, along with the altitude at which they are grown and the conditions of soil and climate at origin, will all affect how the coffee tastes and roasts. However, no combination of these factors will actually lead to great coffee. That is to say, high grown coffee is not better than low grown, nor is the Bourbon strain better than the Geisha. They are simply different and for these reasons it's good to remain open minded and choose coffee on taste alone.

Once green beans have been obtained, sample roasting is the way in which we look for a bean's flavour and quality. Small batches are roasted to the same degree - quite light – so not to allow too much influence from the roast level and let the coffee's natural character shine through. The samples are ground and brewed to the same strength and then 'cupped' or tasted, often blind. The merits or faults of each coffee are noted and discussed, with sweetness, body, mouth feel and acidity evaluated, amongst other things. Importantly, the roaster can decide from these sample roasts what can be done with a particular coffee if bought in bulk. For example, some are earmarked for espresso blend components and others for light roasted filter coffee.

Essentially, a coffee roaster looks to bring out the best and most unique characteristics in a coffee, as well as achieving a good balance of bitters, acidity and sweetness. If there was a mind-blowing chocolate orange hit noted in the cupping session, the roaster will look to develop a roast profile that maximizes those flavours. A roast profile is a record or plan of how much heat was applied to the beans and for how long. Data logging thermometers are used to read the temperature of both the beans and the drum environment during the roast. If saved and brought to the cupping table, they allow us to accurately correlate the taste of the ground, rested beans to the actions we applied in the roasting process. Once a coffee is chosen and a best profile worked out it's time to begin batch roasting.

Having organized the green coffee and preheated the roaster, we put the beans in the hopper and stabilize the heat until it reaches our desired drop temperature. We then pull a tab which drops the beans into a large revolving metal drum with a big gas flame somewhere underneath. The room temperature of the beans drag the drum temperature down as soon as they enter, and we must turn up the gas to get the heat into the beans quickly.

A few minutes into the roast and the beans have gone a bright yellow and give off a straw-like aroma. At this point, moisture is being driven off fast and when this drying phase is complete, the beans will start to turn golden brown and the smell of coffee proper will begin to appear. If the early part of the roast is too slow (cool) the beans will become dried and baked as opposed to roasted and the sugars will not caramelise effectively, leading to lackluster brewed coffee. If the heat is applied too aggressively we may be faced with other problems - the beans can scorch leading to that 'chain store' carbon flavour.

After around seven minutes the beans are a toasty brown and give off wonderful smells. They hit a point called 'first crack' at about nine minutes; a violent and noisy expansion of the beans and a rapid discharge of absorbed heat. By this point we will have worked the gas to maintain our desired profile and must continue to adjust the heat and airflow so the coffee develops in the way we intended. A few minutes after the first crack, a second crack takes place. At this point the coffee is quite dark and we may not want to go this far with many coffees, especially those we have acquired because of a particular or unique flavour.

As the roast progresses and the beans become darker, the batch, when brewed, will take on the flavours of roasting and the characteristics of the individual coffee beans are lost. Towards the end of the roast we monitor the beans' colour, aroma and temperature very closely and small samples are taken from the bean mass to confirm progress. When the roaster judges the batch finished, we pull the door and dump the beans into a big perforated tray through which cool air passes. A sweeper turns, mixing the beans and speeding up the cooling process. It is important to stop the roasting process quickly to prevent the beans from cooking further.

The roasted beans will need a little time to rest, perhaps four days to a week for espresso, less for brewed coffee. This allows carbon dioxide, contained within roasted beans, to escape. Espresso brewed too fresh is extremely gassy making it hard to pull a nice shot, whereas slower brew methods fare better as the gas has had chance to escape. In a month the beans will have become shadows of their fresh roasted glory and so the roaster must get them into the hands and grinders of the brewers and café owners as quickly as possible so they can work their magic.

Coffee roasting is seeing a return to old, before big industry managed to convince the world that vacuum packed coffee could keep for two years and when most towns had a local spinning a *Whitmee* or an *Uno* direct flame roaster at a market stall. It is unlikely that the coffee available at this time would pass muster with today's discerning baristas and customers but with traditional methods combining with new innovation and technology it is an exciting time to be coffee roasting. The world has become a small place and the access we have to coffees and the information about them is amazing. The growing interest in fresh roasted, well sourced coffees in the UK means passionate roasters can share their offerings with equally passionate brewers and coffee lovers, like the cafés listed in this book and their customers.

HARIO | JAPANESE COFFEE EQUIPMENT
YOUR DELICIOUS COFFEE
BREWED TO ORDER

WWW.HARIOGLASS.COM   SALES@BREWEDBYHAND.CO.UK

BREWING METHODS

**A summary of the more commonly used
techniques for brewing coffee.**

Over the last few years, brewed coffee has been making its slow but steady return to the café menu. Furthermore, home brewing coffee is on the increase and there are more great products with which to experiment than ever before. With any type of brewing, it may take some time to find out what method best suits you, but here are a few general tips to help you achieve the best possible results.

For all the methods listed here you will ideally require weighing scales, a grinder, a kettle, a timer and, of course, some delicious coffee. Using freshly ground coffee will always produce a superior brew and be aware that moisture deteriorates coffee, so storing in a fridge or freezer is not advised. Simply keep it in a cool, dry place and use within two weeks of opening.

Always use water between 90 and 94 degrees – that is the ideal temperature range at which to extract coffee. When you boil your kettle let the bubbling disappear – once there are no bubbles in sight, your water should be ready to use. Always heat the vessel you're brewing into as well. If you're using a method with paper filters, be sure to rinse them beforehand as paper will mar the taste of your brewed coffee.

Each brewing method requires a different grind – some fine and some course – and may require some trial and error to perfect. If you're unsure, ask a barista at your local coffee shop for advice. Lastly, always try to time your brews so you can achieve consistency. Ultimately, patience and experimentation are the key to achieving results that satisfy your own palate. With a little dedication and practice, you too can brew great tasting coffee in the comfort of your own home.

CAFETIERE

Also known as the French Press, plunger or coffee press, the cafetiere was patented by Milanese designer Attilio Calimani in 1929 and is perhaps the easiest and cheapest way of brewing coffee at home. Try to use a coarse, even grind, best produced by a burr grinder, with a ratio of 75g per litre of water. Preheat the cafetiere, then add your coffee and cover it with a third of your 90-94 degree water, making sure that all the grounds are covered evenly. Let it sit for thirty seconds, stir and then add the remaining water. Let it 'steep' or brew for 4 minutes before removing the crust of ground coffee on top with a spoon - this lessens the amount of grinds that will end up in your coffee and produces a cleaner taste. Then, placing the filter on top, steadily press down. Remember to decant the coffee quickly to stop any further extraction.

STOVE TOP

Stove tops, also known as moka pots, produce a short drink similar to espresso, though the device employs 1.5 bar of pressure, much less than the 9 bar used in standard espresso machine extractions. The key to brewing a good moka pot is to begin by using boiling water in the bottom chamber - if you start off with cold water, by the time it reaches boiling point you are basically stewing the coffee, over extracting it before the water passes through the grounds. Add and level off medium ground coffee to the basket, drop it into the base chamber, screw on the top and place on a low to medium heat. Listen out for any bubbling or gurgling sounds – as soon as you hear this, remove the moka pot from the heat. To avoid further extraction wrap a cold, wet cloth around the base of the pot to halt the brewing process. Serve and enjoy.

SYPHON FILTER

The syphon filter has become a favoured brewing method amongst baristas in recent years as it can produce a very clean and delicate cup of coffee. Begin by heating water in the lower, spherical chamber using a gas flame or halogen beam heater, making sure that the top half of the syphon rests loosely in place with the filter secured. Once water is above 86 degrees the top chamber should be fully inserted, creating a pressure seal. As the pressure in the bottom chamber increases, the water is sucked up to the top chamber, to which you add your ground coffee - around 14g per 230ml of water. After stirring and roughly 1 minute steeping time, remove the heat. The change in pressure sucks the coffee back down through the filter to the bottom chamber, otherwise known as 'the drop'. Try using a lighter roast coffee in the syphon, as this allows the unique characteristics of the coffee to really shine.

AEROPRESS

Devised in 2005 by Alan Adler, the Aeropress is a simple and versatile way for brewing at home and can be used in a variety of different ways. For the standard Aeropress method using 200ml of water, you are looking to grind between 15 and 18g of coffee with a consistency similar to course sand. Having rinsed the filter paper, rest the Aeropress on top of your cup and add the coffee. Then add enough hot water to cover the coffee, stir and let stand for 30 seconds to pre-infuse. Then add the remaining water and let it steep for a further 30 seconds, making sure to secure the top of the Aeropress in place to create a vacuum. Now begin to plunge, which should take between 20 and 30 seconds. The Aeropress produces a relatively strong coffee, so dilute with hot water if necessary.

DRIP FILTERS

Drip filters are one of the most common ways to brew coffee at home and are also used extensively in cafés throughout London. Be it a cloth, a filter machine or a dripper, the results are what we generally call a black coffee. However, different filters allow different types of extraction and therefore effect the resulting brew. Some drip filters, such as the *V60* (pictured) or the *Chemex*, employ filter papers whereas others use gauze or cloth filters. There are many ways of brewing a dripper but we recommend going with a generic coffee to water ratio of 60g per litre. A medium to fine grind is a good starting point for most drippers but adjust your grind to achieve a two and a half minute extraction time before tweaking to suit you own personal taste. Refer to coffee brewing websites such as *www.brewmethods.com* for links to expert demonstration videos and for specific breakdowns of a variety of drip filter methods.

COFFEE TASTING WHEEL

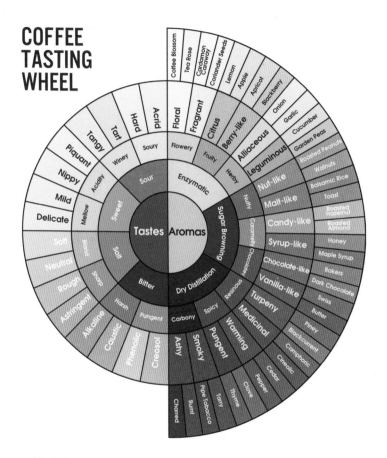

Charts like this are used by professional coffee cuppers in order to assess and grade the individual characteristics of a coffee. It can also be a useful tool for anyone interested in taking their appreciation of coffee to the next level.

DunneFrankowski

www.dunnefrankowski.com

The steady growth of interest in coffee in London has reached a level at which the average consumer demands to know more about the coffee in their cup. By establishing their own creative coffee company offering consultancy and bespoke training, one of the primary aims of entrepeneurs Rob Dunne and Victor Frankowski is to break down the barriers of what is an expansive subject to create an informal, fun and educational experience for all those desirous of knowledge.

Their hugely successful *Sunday Club*, offering courses in Aeropress, brewing and espresso deconstruction at Fitzrovia's highly regarded Tapped & Packed, has engendered further cupping classes in conjunction with the *Disappearing Dining Club*. In a secret location hidden just off busy Old Street, the candlelit ambience of DunneFrankowski's uniquely tailored cupping classes deliver a comprehensive two hour exposition of coffee, covering taste pairing, taste deconstruction and a guided coffee cupping session. Going beyond what we usually perceive and delving into a gastronomical journey, these intimate classes begin with a detailed history and a run-down on the intricacies of aroma, flavour and texture. The table's centrepiece of fruits, chocolates and sweets is used to encourage flavour matching and recognising just a few of the 800 aromatic compounds that have so far been discovered in coffee. Designed for all levels of expertise, the DunneFrankowski experience is an ideal place to begin your own coffee journey and to appreciate what goes into your favourite cup of coffee.

With an impressive fifteen years shared experience, having learnt their service and coffee craft as baristas in high-profile specialty coffee shops, DunneFrankowski is the first company of its kind in the capital and has its finger on the pulse of café culture, symbolising the current swathe of young Londoners thriving in a city with its own ample traditions in both coffee and gastronomy.

COFFEE GLOSSARY

A list of terms commonly used within the coffee industry.

ACIDITY
One of the three principal tastes employed by professional coffee tasters in detailing a particular coffee or blend. When used in coffee terms acidity is a desirable characteristic, providing a bright, vibrant quality.

AMERICANO
(*Caffè Americano*)
A term coined during World War II when American GIs stationed in Europe would add hot water to their espresso to replicate the coffee they were accustomed to drinking in the United States. Essentially the term still means an espresso with added hot water.

ARABICA (*Coffea Arabica*)
The most widely grown species of coffee tree, Arabica accounts for approximately 70% of the world's coffee and thrives when grown at high elevation in cooler and dryer climates. It is generally seen as superior in terms of taste and quality to other coffee species. The plant was originally indigenous to Ethiopia but the name Arabica is derived from the Arabian Peninsula, having been exported there in large quantities. It is believed to be the first coffee species to be cultivated, with evidence of its growth dating back well over 1000 years.

BARISTA
The Italian term for *bar person* which now connotes a professional espresso machine operator.

BLEND
A combination of two or more coffee subspecies (such as Bourbon or Typica) that are blended together. It can lead to a more balanced coffee flavour or flavours that are greater than the sum total of its parts.

BODY
Describes the heaviness of the coffee on the tongue when tasted (for example thin, watery, oily, thick or syrupy).

BREW TIME
Contact time between water and coffee. The guideline for a correctly brewed espresso is between 20 and 30 seconds, though the exact times are dictated by roasting dates, blend components and many other variables.

CORTADO
A traditional Spanish coffee made up of an espresso shot cut with a small amount of steamed milk without much foam. A Spanish piccolo.

CREMA
The golden foam that covers the surface of an espresso shot. Crema is made by the pressurised brew water forcing its way through the coffee bed.

CUPPING
The procedure employed by coffee tasters in order to evaluate samples of coffee beans, the key evaluation characteristics being aroma, acidity, body and flavour.

DOSAGE
The amount of ground coffee used to produce an espresso shot. Typically around 7-11 grams of coffee is used for a single espresso shot and 16-25 grams for a double.

ESPRESSO
The basis of most coffee beverages served in cafés, an espresso shot is produced when hot water is forced at high pressure through a compressed bed of finely ground coffee in an espresso machine. This generally takes between 20 and 30 seconds and yields 20-30 mls of liquid. Much like the English word 'express', the term refers to the speed of its preparation (compared to other coffee brewing methods) and also conveys 'expressly' or 'just for you.'

FLAT WHITE
An espresso based beverage invented in Australia or New Zealand prepared by pouring steamed milk with a thin layer of microfoam over a single or double shot of espresso.

GRIND
Whole coffee beans are ground to different sizes depending on the brew method. As a rule the longer the brew time, the larger or courser the grind. So, the espresso grind is small or fine and takes up to approximately 30 seconds, whereas the cafetiere grind is coarser and is brewed for approximately 4 minutes.

LATTE (*Caffè Latte*)
Literally translated from the Italian for 'coffee and milk', a latte is a single espresso shot combined with foamed milk and is usually served in a glass.

LATTE ART
The creation of a pattern or design on the surface of a coffee beverage by either free pouring steamed milk over an espresso shot or etching designs onto the finished coffee using a coffee stirrer. Common types of latte art are the Rosetta or the heart shape.

MICRO-LOT COFFEES
A small lot of coffee that has benefited from conditions, such as soil, shade or selective picking, that has been isolated in one particular area of a farm. These conditions can create a unique character to the coffee which sets it apart from the rest of the crop in terms of quality. Due to the extra preparation required, their resulting quality and the small scale of their production, micro-lot coffees also fetch higher prices.

OVER EXTRACTED

Bitter, harsh and unpleasant flavours that are the result of the contact time between water and coffee grounds being too long or brew water that is too hot.

PICCOLO

Literally meaning 'small' in Italian, a Piccolo is a smaller variant of the latte. Consists of an espresso or ristretto shot, topped with steamed milk and is usually served in a small glass at a 1:1 ratio of espresso to milk.

RISTRETTO

A "restricted" espresso. A ristretto is richer and more intense than a traditional espresso shot due to the smaller volume of brew water in comparison to coffee.

ROBUSTA (*Coffea Canephora*)

Behind Arabica, Robusta is the other primary coffee species to be used commercially. Unlike Arabica, Robusta has a shallow root system and grows a robust tree or shrub that is less susceptible to pests and disease, requires less care in growing and can flourish at low altitudes. The typical yield of Robusta is twice that of Arabica and the resulting coffee contains twice as much caffeine, though less complex flavours. Robusta is often used as a filler in lower-quality filter blends and instant coffees.

SINGLE ORIGIN COFFEE

Coffee from one country. Single origin coffees can capture the essence of a particular country due to variants such as soil, altitude and climate specific to that growing area. Within single origin definitions there are also single estate coffees, which refers to an area or estate within that country of origin, akin to wine regions.

SPECIALTY COFFEE

A term used to denote a gourmet or premium coffee that has achieved a 'specialty' classification having scored 80 points or above on the one hundred point grading scale employed by traders and coffee associations. Specialty coffee has also come to represent a wider range of meaning, encompassing methods of coffee preparation, industry practice and café culture

TAMP/TAMPING

The method by which loose coffee grounds are compressed and compacted into a portafilter basket in preparation for brewing espresso.

UNDER EXTRACTED

When contact time, temperature or turbulence is insufficient to fully extract desirable flavours from coffee.

Thanks

A.J. Kinnell, Nick and Andrew Tolley, Lawrence Sinclair, Rob Dunne,
Derek Lamberton, Bahar Tafti, Paul Radin, Steven Macatonia,
Jeremy Torz, Ben Townsend, James Hoffmann, Richard Reed,
Jeremy Challender, James Phillips, Lewin Chalkley, Peter Dore-Smith,
Matt Buckley, Cameron McClure, Fabio Ferreira, Lizzy Parle,
Jess Seaton, Demelza Donohoo, Ross Brown, Will Riley,
Nick Coates, George Wallace, Kurt Stewart, Elisa Kelly,
Tim d'Offay, Mark Lamberton

We also appreciate the help and wisdom of: Richard Grills, B.P. Evans,
Susan & Robin Sykes, Karen, Meg, Holly, Mr. Smith, Rachael, Cal,
Taras, Al Tomlins, all at Marwood, Taylor St., Ground, Small Batch and
Coffee@33 in Brighton, Dan Jones aka Electronic Dog, Dominic Vacher
and the team at Four Corners, Anton, John and Adam @ Waterstones.

And to all the café owners, coffee roasters and baristas who have
made us feel so welcome over the past 12 months, this book is for you.

Maps

On the following pages you will find detailed and comprehensive maps of London. Using the nearest tube & rail stations, as well as landmarks and major roads, they will help you to find all the cafés featured in this book.

Each of the five areas is represented by its own page, with the more outlying cafés to the east, north & south displayed as small maps simply showing the café and the nearest access by train.

KEY

≥ - Train Station

1 - Café

⊖ - Underground Station

2 - Coffee Cart

⊖ - Overground Station

The City

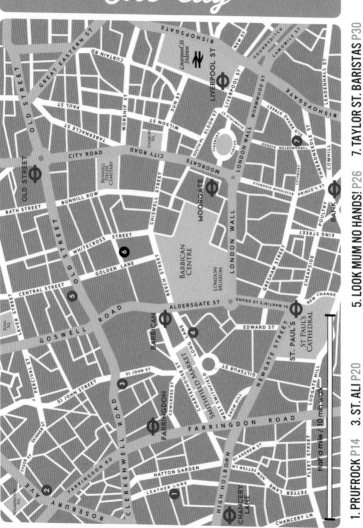

Half a mile / 10 min walk

1. PRUFROCK P14
2. CARAVAN P18
3. ST. ALI P20
4. DOSE ESPRESSO P24
5. LOOK MUM NO HANDS! P26
6. GIDDY UP P28
7. TAYLOR ST. BARISTAS P30

West End

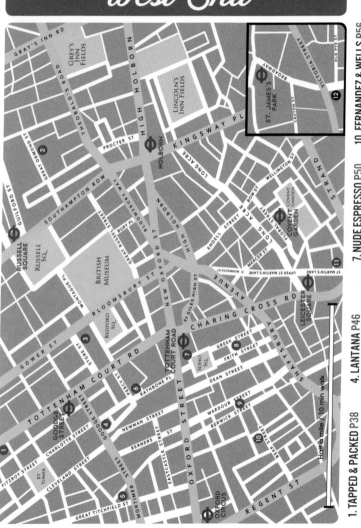

Half a mile / 10 min walk